Aren't You Glad That It's Not
Christmas Everyday?

Memoirs of a Wizzard Drummer

by

Charlie Grima
*Ex Drummer of Roy Wood's Wizzard*

Published by: Mirag Publications, UK

ISBN Number : 978-0-9931877-1-1

# TABLE OF CONTENTS

# SPECIAL THANKS

I would like to thank the following people for their encouragement and support in writing this Memoir:

**Malcolm & Sue Bell, Lynda & Lyndsay, Tony & Hazel, Mike & Karrie.**

Thank You to **Terry Cohen** for her time and effort.

Also, **Mike Ottely** for his permission to use his photo for the front cover. **Mike** is a friend and official photographer of the group and took loads of photos in the 3 year lifespan of **Wizzard**.

**Megan Davies** for her time and help.

**Billy Clarke** for the photo of the W.K. Jump Band.

**Martin Kinch** for all his help.

A real big Thank You to **Christine Clayfield**, who kindly gave her valuable time to format it all and get it published.
Lastly apologies to anyone who has not been mentioned.
But I am allowed a senior moment or two surely?
CG.

# MALTA

36 Poala Square, Poala, Malta.
That was our family address where I lived up to the age
of ten. As well as being our home it was also a bar/café
called Mackay Bar.
It was run by my father, Salvo, and my mother, Maria,
but we all mucked in together generally.
The name Mackay came from a ship that my father had
worked on in the Merchant Navy.

We used to serve tea, coffee, beer, ice cream and
homemade lemon sorbet which my father used to make.
I used to love watching him make it.
He and Mum also made light snacks, two of which
were Pastitzi and Cassatta.
These are indigenous to the island. Pastitzi is a sort of
boat-shaped puff-pastry filled with either ricotta cheese
or mashed peas and finely chopped fried onions and the
latter (although it sounds like the Italian ice cream) was
also a pastry snack, round in shape, thicker pastry filled
with ricotta cheese.
I sometimes woke up around 5am and helped Pop to
make them. You can still get them from street-vendors
now. They're a delicious snack.

My childhood…it was quite a happy one I suppose, as
far as most childhoods go.
There was one major upset however, and that was the
death of my younger baby brother Lelli; he died of
pneumonia. I was about four at the time. I can't
remember any details. It's all very vague.

We had a well in the backyard, which we used as a
fridge. We filled the bucket with bottles of pop, beer,
wine etc. Then we'd lower it till we'd feel it touch the
water at the bottom. It stayed there for a day or two,
sometimes longer. It worked.

At that age I really believed that there was a 'Sarena' (a sort of witch) living at the bottom. I'm not quite sure where the myth came from exactly but in later years I found out that it was a made up story to act as a deterrent to stop us kids from leaning too far over and falling in. (I know what you're thinking, how cruel) Well! Pardon the pun. It certainly worked.

As Malta is predominantly a Catholic country, most activities took place in or around the church.
I was an altar boy and generally helped around at our local Church. It was a huge place - most churches are, in Malta.
One incident that is quite memorable, I suppose, was on bell-ringing duty.
(You can just picture the scene I'd pull the rope, and on the return I would leave the ground by about four inches). One day the rope snapped and came crashing down on my head; I was overcome with a mixture of guilt, because of the damage I may have done, but also fright, because I expected this ruddy great big bell to follow the rope.
I would not go near the belfry for days after that.
How did you cope Quasimodo?

Because Malta is blessed with a very warm climate most pursuits took place outdoors. In the summer months at school, classes would be held outside in the shade. At night, if it was unbearably hot, I would sleep either on the roof (as they are generally all flat), or the little balcony above our front door. It was quite tiny and it was a bit of an adventure really. A bit like here in the UK when some kids sleep in tents in the back garden but this had its drawbacks during market day, as you were woken up about five in the morning, with the noise of the market-traders setting up their stalls right across the road.

My father eventually had to shut up shop as business wasn't good and he later emigrated to England; Birmingham to be precise. My two eldest brothers Joey and Johnny went with him. They all ended up working for British Rail at Tyseley station (those were the days when trains ran on time).

After about a year or so there, he sent for us ...that is, myself, my mum, brother Salvo and my sister, Wenza.

I remember the day before we were to fly to England very well, because it was Mum's birthday, August 2nd. The date we emigrated was 3rd August 1955.
Mum had cooked a couple of rabbits in the traditional Maltese way. 'Stuffatt'... (stew in English) cooked in red wine, peas, onions and of course, garlic. As always it was delicious. We ate on the beach of our favourite haunt, a place called Bir-Zebbugga.
I remember being both sad, and at the same time, excited about leaving.
I had been to Luqa airport several times before, because my brother-in-law was stationed there in the RAF and I sometimes visited him. The plane we were to board was a Viscount - a four-prop craft. I could feel the excitement building up as I crossed the tarmac; up the steps we went. Of course I had the window-seat and we took off very shortly after.
We made one stop in Nice, France, for re –fuelling. They let us off the plane and we went to the cafeteria. I remember my brother being astonished at the price we were charged for an orange juice - it seemed really steep compared to Maltese prices.

It wasn't long before we were off again, Heathrow-bound.
From the moment the wheels touched down, my head began reeling with a mixture of excitement and anticipation.

I had seen stairs before, but never ones that move, and I'd seen pictures of big red buses in books, and here I was about to board one. Of course I made a beeline for the stairs to the top deck and sat in the front.

We got off at Paddington as we were going to spend that night at the hotel next to the station in Praed Street. We spent most of the next day in and around the hotel going for a short stroll, trying to take everything in, like traffic lights and zebra-crossings. What are these things? ...We didn't have these things in Malta.

Almost everything we saw was a revelation.

What a culture shock!!!

That night we caught the train to Birmingham, which was to become our new home.

So this is what a real train looks like? I remember I used to have a picture book with drawings of a train in a station, but I had never actually seen one for real until now.

There was steam everywhere and the noise was terrific. Off we went chugging along to Brum, as I now affectionately call it.

Dad was renting a couple of rooms in this place on the Pershore Road and we were to stay there for quite a few months.

That's when I started to get a little homesick, but it didn't last too long. My brother Salvo and I became friendly with the people who lived across the road and we used to get asked over for tea and watch TV. Yes you could probably imagine, we sat about a foot away from the screen totally mesmerised by the whole thing. They had one of those magnifying glasses that you screwed to the screen front to enlarge the picture. Who would have thought that, years later, I would be appearing on this very same contraption, but I'll come to that later.

My school days were an education (excuse the pun) in themselves. At first I used to 'talka lika dis' but it didn't take long to develop a full-blooded 'Brummie' accent, which I still can't completely shake off.

I used to get teased about my name 'Carmello' so I soon adopted my second name of Charles.

I was christened (wait for it) Carmello, Charles, Joseph, Francis, Anthony. They do tend to do that in most Mediterranean countries.

We moved around quite a bit, so I attended a few schools, all Catholic of course. I won't bore you by naming all of them so I'll skip to the last one, which was St Michael's in Flood Street, Digbeth. It was right round the corner from the Bird's Custard factory.

Just thinking about it now, I can still imagine the smell around there; that vanilla aroma that hung around the area.

All in all I did all right at school; the couple of subjects that I seemed to do well in were: English and Geography. I left school at 15.

My first job was as an apprentice joiner with a firm called J.R Pearson, which my brother-in law Len got for me.

I wanted to be a carpenter, well, joiner to be precise. I loved working with wood; there was a time when I could identify various types of wood.

The firm arranged for me to go to college once a week. I attended Brooklyn Technical College in Great Barr, for three years.

We were then living at 63 Gough Road, Edgbaston.

Next-door to us, lived another Maltese man who was known affectionately as 'uncle.' He had lodgers there who were all Maltese. I can't quite remember names, but they were real characters (they wouldn't have looked out of place in a Scorsese movie).

It was about this period in time that we discovered that my eldest brother Joe was suffering from a nervous breakdown, which got gradually worse, and later turned into schizophrenia.

We were all at a loss as how to handle it; the anguish and pain of it was that no one knew exactly what caused it.

He was admitted into All Saints Hospital, in Winson Green for quite a long period.

They gave him electric-shock treatment and experimented with different drugs and medication, which had horrible side effects.

He was eventually discharged and carried on as a day-patient for a long while, then gradually he spent more time at home, going for his injection once a month up until the day he died from a massive heart-attack.

I have left out many depressing details so as not to bore or depress you too much.

It was also whilst we were at this address that my father died. He dropped dead in the street very early one morning on his way to work.

I was with Mum in Didcot, Oxfordshire at the time where Kitty, my eldest sister lived.

Mum and I were staying with her because she'd just had a baby, and Mum went there to help for a few days. They were tough times.

My sister Kitty emigrated to Australia and she has seven grown up kids now.

I'm in touch with one of her daughters, Sandy, by e-mail and she keeps me informed with news about the family. So I'm a great uncle.

## I'VE GOT RHYTHM

I suppose you could say the first signs of my rhythmical-tendencies came through when I used to listen to Edmundo Ross on Saturday mornings.
He was a bandleader of a Latin American band.

I used to get two forks from the kitchen and play along on the edge of the bed, which used to drive the rest of the family mad.

The fact that it was a metal-framed bed didn't help much to alleviate the noise.

Eventually, I started to look forward to Saturdays, becoming more confident each week.

We eventually moved to an area of Birmingham, called Nechells just down the road from Saltley (or if you're a Brummie… Soltloy).

We lived on the third floor of a block of flats called Greenbank House; there was a medical centre on the ground floor which took up half of the 'L' shaped building.

I used to hang around two places in Nechells. One was Bloomsbury Street School Hall, which became a youth club a couple of days a week, and the other was Nechells Green Community Centre.

The latter is still there in Melvina Road.

That is where it all started for me really. I was quite a keen dancer - jiving as it was called then (what a great word) and I looked forward to Thursdays, because that's when they had a live group playing there. They had a girl vocalist and they called themselves Toni Martell & The Interns (none of them had anything to do with the medical profession). I think it was a TV programme of that time but don't quote me on that. After all, we're talking '62'/63 here.

They played Shadow's hits, early Beatles and the Kinks. I was there every week rocking away, and if I wasn't jiving, I'd be tapping on something or other.

The Interns consisted of:

Ivan Adams...lead guitar/vocals, Malcolm Bell...bass guitar/vocals... Jimmy Walpole...rhythm guitar/vocals… Toni Martell, (real name Annie Butler vocals) and Duke...drums.

There were a couple of times when
Duke couldn't make it to the booking, as a gig was then
called, but his drums were already set up by a friend of
the boys and on one occasion they asked me to
play...Well! I froze on the spot. 'I can't play those
things,' I said, or something to that effect...Well, with a
little persuasion and lots of encouragement, I climbed
up on the little stage and sat behind the kit. The only
beat I could muster, was the beat from The Shadows
hit, 'Apache.'

I've got to be honest, I did get an amazing sensation
from it all and as I'm being honest, I was looking
forward to the next opportunity.
At that time I was working at Bridge Street Garage off
Broad Street, helping out with light mechanical work,
serving petrol, washing cars etc. All this time I was still
having the occasional 'sit-in' with the boys, and they
encouraged me to get myself a drum kit.
So I started looking around for one, and before long I
spotted a white, mother-of-pearl 'OLMYPIC' kit for
£80.

Now £80 doesn't sound a lot in this day and age but
back then it was a small fortune. It took me over a year
to pay it off on the old hire purchase.
I used to go along with my little paying-in book every
Saturday to Ringway Music and I'd pay Lionel Rubin
my weekly instalment. Lionel was one of my first
influences; he was a jazz drummer and I used to watch
him on Lunch Box with the Jerry Allen Trio, featuring
a singer and actress Noel Gordon (Crossroads).

I remember going for lessons, but I only attended the
first two. They dealt mainly with stick holding, and a
couple of 'rudiments.'
I guess I was too impatient. I just wanted to get out
there and play.

Before I knew it Duke was leaving the group as he was more into jazz.

So the boys asked me to rehearse with them and of course I was delighted!

Gradually I became more and more confident as we rehearsed, and soon I found myself doing real gigs.

We played twice a week: once at the Nechells Green Community Centre and the other at the Bloomsbury School Youth Club.

Our only mode of transport then was an old clapped out pram, which we used to push from Ivan's house loaded with our stuff across the green to these two places.

If I remember rightly the money then was something like seven pounds for the two gigs, (wait!)...between us that is!

Then eventually we moved on to weddings, the odd pub etc. We played mostly on weekends and were still semi-pro.

Sorry to digress, but, I've just remembered one particular evening. There was a knock on my door and one of the guys in this band that I was in (name escapes me) said, 'We've got a booking and they're paying us £10.'

I remember thinking Wow!!! That's good money.

I think we were replacing a group that failed to show up therefore it was a last minute thing.

So off we went to this gig and when we got there the place was packed. So we had to set up in front of the audience, which was a weird feeling. Eventually we set up and we were ready to go.

To stop my bass drum from moving we had put a speaker in front of it. Well!!! You can guess what's coming next...

We started with Chuck Berry's 'Johnny Be Good.' After the famous guitar intro all hell broke loose. The speaker that was supposed to stop my bass drum from moving, didn't and it went crashing on to an amplifier -

the type with all the valves showing and of course it went up in a puff of smoke and that was the start and end of the gig.

The promoter came on stage and said something like, 'Come back when you've got better equipment lads.'

Then he instructed the DJ to stick more dance tracks on and turn the volume up.

Meanwhile we had to humbly pack our gear away and make our way through the crowd as we went out.

'Gutted' is one way of describing how we all felt, me especially.

It was very early in my career but it was still embarrassing.

Sorry for the diversion - back to my first ever band, The Interns.

Before I had joined the group they used to go down to Torquay to a holiday-camp called Barton Hall for a holiday, but they would take the equipment with them and play a couple of nights a week, whilst on holiday there.

Needless to say I found it quite adventurous the first time I went down there with them.

Our transport by then was Malcolm's dad's van; it was an old Commer LD I think.

A guy called Ray Miller, a nice guy with a dry sense of humour became our manager.

All of this was of course on a semi-professional basis.

Meanwhile we all had day jobs. I know that Malcolm and Ivan were lift engineers and they were still in those jobs until they both retired quite recently.

I was in the joiner job for around three years then after that I had quite a variety of day jobs including, guillotine operator in a steel works, removals, (2 days) industrial window cleaner, storekeeper's assistant and a few more besides which I can't remember or quite frankly don't want to remember!

A scrap-metal dealer named Gordon who fancied himself as a bit of an entrepreneur, managed the band later. One residency that he got us was in a nightclub in Walsall. One night that stands out is the night Malcolm's mum came with us. A gig was more of a family affair in those days. We had no idea that we were meant to back a stripper that night. We hadn't seen her up until the moment that she walked on the stage.

Now, I don't want to seem unkind but if I said that she had passed her sell-by date as a stripper it should give you an idea of her age.

To add to our rapidly increasing embarrassment she started her routine but she had difficulty in removing her skirt, so she used Malcolm's mum's shoulder to lean on, to steady herself.

Well! You can imagine, we were all cracking up with laughter, except Malcolm, of course. He crouched down behind this big plant, which luckily for him, was conveniently placed at the back of the tiny stage. I was dreading her coming to me. I was pissing myself laughing at the whole scenario.

I'm glad to say we didn't do that gig for much longer. We later parted company from Gordon and a short while later, Annie left the band. She eventually went to live in Norway.

We had quite a little following; some of the people that come to mind are:

Ken, who later married Gladys (Gladys was my jiving partner).

We were a bit hot on that dance floor I can tell you!

'Winkie' of course; who could forget 'Winkie?' He was our 'roadie' way before the word was even heard of. He was one of the few guys around at the time with long hair. His real name was Raymond Winkett.

And there were also characters like 'Tucker', Eddie, Sherry, Pattie, The Valentti's...I'd better stop, I'm bound to leave someone out.

I remember that we were a little nervous about the Group-Competition that was coming up in the next few days. It was held at The West End, a dance hall in what was then Suffolk Street. It was known for its springy floor.

There were about nine groups in all.

Much to our surprise we came third. The only two others that I remember, were 'The Everglades' fronted by Trevor Burton, (who later found fame with The Move).

He has his own band now and is still rocking around Brum.

There was also a band called Monopoly, which later became The Raymond Froggatt Band, fronted by the legendary Raymond Froggatt, singer, songwriter of such hits as: 'Callow La Vita', a hit for Dave Clarke Five, 'Roly,' 'Big Ship' (a hit for Cliff Richard) and a host of others.

I like to think of him as the 'Bard of Brum.'

The Everglades came first and Monopoly second if I remember right.

It was not long after that contest that we met up with the late John Killigrew. He was a very talented guitarist/singer. He was the greatest influence on us – almost like a musical Guru.

I remember he had the very first Gibson Les Paul guitar we had ever seen. He was into Carl Perkins, Chuck Berry and he had that authentic rock sound as well. His versatility was astonishing. He was an even better jazz guitarist.

It was he who introduced me to the sounds of guitarists like: Wes Montgomery, Barney Kessell and Charlie Byrd to name just a few.

His singing was also something else. He could impersonate people like Sinatra, Tony Bennett, Johnny Mathis, Nat King Cole, and Bobby Darin.

He occasionally had a sit-in with us as he lived in Cato Street, just around the corner from the Community Centre.

Eventually the Interns kind of splintered into another group and we called ourselves The Villains.
The line-up for that band was John Killigrew, (guitar/vocals and front man), Guy (guitar), Alan Powell (bass guitar/vocals), Richard Lonnen (organ) and yours truly (drums).

That was the very first band I went abroad with and I remember we were quite excited about it.
The small tour of Germany was of the 'Star Palast' club circuit; there were a few of these places scattered around Northern Germany. The first stop was Keil.
I remember as we pulled up outside this place, we all gulped. It looked a bit run down, in fact I distinctly remember John Killigrew (who was at the wheel of the van) saying, "What a hole," or something stronger, and we were about to turn around and head back home to the UK when out came the promoter and asked:
"You are Ze Willians Yes?"
We then realised that was it! We were committed.

The other clubs were dotted around Germany, Rendsburg, Eckernförde and Lüneburg.
I can't remember all the other places, but it was an eye opening experience.

The first difference we noticed was the amount of sets we were asked to play. I mean in the UK when you do a pub, the most you do is 2 sets and finish just after 11pm - in some places before that, depending on the landlord.
With these places in Germany you started between 7pm or 8pm and did 45minute sets with a 15- minute break right up until 2am or 3am.

It wasn't too bad if there was another band on as well, because you shared the sets, but if you were the only band, then you needed to have a huge repertoire.
The promoter was known for not paying bands regularly.
One time I was so broke that I had to sell my rings and in those days I had one on each finger, (except the thumbs - I can't stand to see rings on thumbs) just so I could get a Goulash supper.
You learnt numbers as you went along. On the whole it was a good experience - a bit of an apprenticeship really, after all it didn't do The Beatles any harm now did it?

However we did get ripped off on our first visit.
After that, bands came and went. I can only recall a few. Let's see now there was: Combined Action, Organised Chaos, The Block with not one, but two vocalists. Kirk St James and Brenda Bosworth who sounded and looked just like Brenda Lee.
We gigged around the country, played a couple of US Air force bases, plus most pubs in the Midlands.
The American Air Force bases were a regular source of work for most bands.

In spite of the fact that these American bases were scattered over the UK once you entered the base you were theoretically on American soil. You were bound by their rules and regulations. Most of the ones I did were fine. You tended to get treated well. If you wanted to buy a packet of cigarettes for instance you had to get one of the guys in the force to get them for you.

Then came 'Hannibal' again with Kirk St James, one of my oldest buddies. A terrific performer: a front man and the ultimate showman ( he's still in touch). The guitarist in that band was Adrian Ingram, who was, and still is, a very dedicated musician.

He received a diploma from The London College of
Music, an out and out jazz musician and tutor.
Together, we played Germany and Holland. There was
a lot of improvising in that band, freedom to express
yourself. When it worked it was a pleasure.
We did a few small festivals over there and
the audiences seemed more appreciative and
enthusiastic towards the artist.

## SCENE SHIFTING

In 1968 I worked at the Alexandra Theatre in
Birmingham as a stagehand and scene shifter.
I loved it; the atmosphere under the stage was great and
we would play cards while listening out for our next
cue and at the given time we all went to our designated
part of the wings to get ready to change the scenery.
They were called 'flats' if I remember right. I equally
enjoyed 'get ins' and 'get outs.' We would work right
through the night taking all the scenery down from one
show and tidying up the stage and getting it ready for
the 'get in' of the next show. It was a team effort. One
of the fellow workers there was Paul Henry, who later
found fame as an actor in the TV soap Crossroads. He
played Benny, always wore a woollen hat and he was
one of the central characters for a long time.

The shows varied from a straight drama or The London
Festival Ballet Company and towards Christmas we got
ready for a Pantomime.

It was fun and it gave me an insight into the workings
of a professional theatre.

## JAZZ & CIDER

I used to go to Erdington with a bunch of pals from
Nechells to a pub called 'The Roebuck' to listen to

some Traditional Jazz. I got into cider there and although I couldn't drink a huge quantity, it was good stuff. A pint and a half was my limit.

I used to watch the drummer like a hawk. I was impressed by it all.

On one occasion when the band had their break between sets, these two guys got up on stage.

They were introduced as coming from London, (but the announcer got it wrong).

One guy played guitar, and the other played piano and guitar.

They played mainly blues.

Then the guy on piano went into a Ray Charles classic, 'Georgia On My Mind' and his voice actually made the hairs on the back of my neck stand up. How could such a soulful voice come from a white guy?

He was Stevie Winwood and the guitarist was Spencer Davis.

Who would have known then that later, much later, I would be sharing a stage with them and the rest of the Spencer Davis Group at Alexandra Palace in Wizzard? I got to know Pete York the drummer. He is very technical - a great jazzer. He now lives in Germany and I e-mail him from time to time.

There were a few bands on that night one of which was 'The Real Thing'.

**The Wellington Kitch Jump Band** (now there's a name and a half) was a 7-piece soul band with a very gifted front man named John Howells.

John was previously with a band called The 'N'Betweens' with Noddy Holder and after John left, they became Ambrose Slade then finally Slade.

As well as touring up and down the country on our own, we also backed some American soul artistes such as: 'The Impressions' and Garnett Mimms, to name just a couple.

Not many people have heard of Garnet but he was a true professional.

Garnet is an American singer, influential in soul music and rhythm and blues. He first achieved success as the lead singer of Garnet Mimms and The Enchanters, and is best known for the 1963 hit 'Cry Baby' later recorded by Janis Joplin.

He toured the UK frequently and he always asked for us to back him when he came over.

We got on great with him.

He had this old fashioned patter when introducing an up tempo number; he used to say…"*You know when I was younger, my Pa used to say to me son, when you get older go and have yourself some fun. Well! I'm three times seven, that makes me twenty one, you know what to do Charlie*"

And that was my cue to count in the number.

It was always a pleasure to work with him.

As the Kitch, we went to Zurich for a month. The gig was the Hirschen Hotel which was a well known gig in the area - loads of English bands worked there, for instance there were a couple of bands from Brum that did it: 'Breakthru' a blues outfit, all pals of mine, their lead singer Gary Aflalo who I'm still in touch with, and later was responsible for me getting into acting, as I will explain later. Another Brum band that played there was 'Earth' ('Black Sabbath').

In those days there used to be 'all nighters'. Usually on a weekend, you would have a few bands playing literally through the night. I remember doing quite a few with various bands. There was one at Coventry Locarno with 'Pink Floyd'. They had just released 'See Emily Play.' Later there was one at the Steering Wheel Club in West Bromwich. That was with 'The Spencer Davis Group' and 'Cream' (Eric Clapton, Jack Bruce and Ginger Baker).

There was also one in London at the 'Flamingo Club' in Wardour Street. We were knackered by the time we actually finished and loaded up. All we wanted to do was sleep but we still had a two and a half hour journey home, longer if you were the poor bugger who was dropped off last.

I used to like a venue in Droitwich Spa, Worcestershire called The Chateau Impney. It is a magnificent bit of architecture; I remember doing an all nighter there with Jimmy Cliff topping the bill.

Whenever we played London there were a load of clubs in those days, places like 'Scotch of St James', 'The Speakeasy'.

'The Bag 'O' Nails', 'The Flamingo', 'Tiles' and of course 'The Whisky Agogo'. These names won't mean much to many people but if you're a musician over the age of 50, then you would have played at least one of them.

One hotel that most of the bands stayed in was 'The Maddison Hotel' on Sussex Gardens just off the Edgware Road. It was actually two hotels next door to each other.

Because most of its guests were bands the breakfast period was a considerably longer time than other hotels simply because bands came in a lot later than other guests and they weren't going to get up early for breakfast.

The dining room walls were completely covered with signed photos of bands. I remember one time when Joe Cocker and his band were actually living there for a short while.

The car park was always full of Ford Transits.

Well! It was cheap and cheerful.

We later became The Cedar Set. Same outfit, but the reason for the name change was because we became the resident band in The Cedar Club, one of the most popular nightclubs in Birmingham at the time.

Actually the name on the side of the van was spelt Cedar Cet and to this day I don't know if it was intentional or a balls up on the sign writer's behalf.

Eddie Fewtrell, a well-known businessman and entrepreneur and one of many brothers, owned the Cedar Club. Most of them were in the nightclub business too. He was affectionately known as 'The King of Clubs'.

He later went on to open several clubs in Birmingham: Rebbeca's, Barbarella's and Abigail's.

I think that the clubs were named after his daughters but I'm not a hundred percent sure.

Whilst we were resident at the Cedar Club there was a time when we were allowed to go and do two weeks at the Playboy Club in London.

What a strange place. They had so many stipulations and silly rules, for example, when you finished a set you couldn't go and drink in the bar where you had just played, but you could go to your dressing room. Well! I've seen bigger cupboards than that so called dressing room. The other place you could go to was the canteen, which was only slightly bigger. There you could help yourself to free food but you could not fraternise with the Bunny girls.

There was one Bunny girl who was Australian and she didn't care much for the stupid rules and she used to get a pack of cards out and sit with us and play.

Oh! I almost forgot! We weren't allowed to go in the front entrance - we had to use the side door and go through the kitchens.

We used to use the tube or the bus to get to the club and leave our van parked at the hotel because our gear was already set up.

One night we were running a bit late so we caught a taxi and the taxi stopped outside the front entrance. The doorman, dressed in his commissioner's outfit, came to open the door to the cab but when he saw it was us musicians, he very quickly let go of the door.

His face was a picture!

As part of our residency deal, Eddie became our Manager.

He bought us all suits and a Transit van, with the name emblazoned on both sides.

When we became residents at 'The Cedar' we supported all the stars that appeared at the club, stars such as: Ben E King, Duane Eddy, Solomon Burke, Booker T & The MGs, Junior Walker & the All Stars ('How sweet it is to be loved by you') and others like: Status Quo, in their early days (they had just released their first hit, ('Pictures of Matchstick Men'), 'The Walker Bros', 'Steampacket' (Who? I hear you say).They were an R&B outfit with Long John Baldry, Rod Stewart and Julie Driscoll - vocals, Brian Auger - organ, Vic Briggs - guitar, Richard Brown - bass guitar, and Micky Waller – drums.

If you're under forty you probably won't have heard of them.


We had just added a brilliant guitarist, he was Vernon Perrera. He had an amazing stage presence; he looked a bit like Prince.

The women used to go nuts over him. He was into blues and he had a good voice too. He would emulate Hendrix by playing with his teeth during a solo.

When we eventually split up a couple of years later Vernon went on to form another band called Possessed. Sadly he died in a van crash along with two other members of the band. That was a sad day for us Brummies.

I remember doing a benefit gig at Barbarella's in the big room, on the big stage which was just as well as there were fifteen or more musicians on there at one time. It was quite a moving gig as we ended it with 'Knocking on Heaven's Door.'

Around that time The Move were an up and coming band; they frequented the club and most of the time they would get up on our gear and do a couple of numbers.

The Birmingham music scene in those days was really thriving, and we musicians were all like a big family. We still are in a way; even now whenever I go and visit, I meet up with the old faces, some are still playing, and some have quit the music game and earning good money instead.

I later landed a residency at Barbarella's with my very dear old friend Kirk St James. The place was huge. It had several different rooms and the main acts were always in the biggest room and on the biggest stage. We played in the smaller room just off the main room. The whole place used to get packed.

We were there for only a short time and then we went our separate ways but I'm still in touch with Kirk from time to time.

Led Zeppelin was another up and coming band at the time and John Bonham and Robert Plant used to come in the club. Bonzo, (as Bonham is affectionately known) was the loudest drummer in the whole of the Midlands. That doesn't take anything away from his technique. He was one of my idols as Rock drummers go.

He used to really give my kit a thrashing, so much so that he would inevitably put a skin through, but he always gave me a couple of quid after, to get another skin the next day.

Robert Plant I knew from way back before Zeppelin. He was the front man vocalist with a soul outfit called 'Listen'.

I'm not quite sure which band I was in then. It could have been a band called 'Combined Action.' We were on the same bill at a venue in the town centre - a ballroom above the Co-op in the High Street.

He seemed to like a tie that I was wearing, and I liked a belt that he was wearing, so we made a swop. He later got more into blues. He was always going to be a star; even in those early days you could tell.

We were then managed by Chas Peate, and at one time our singer /front man left, and he brought Robert to try it out with us.

I distinctly remember the song he sang and it was 'Ain't Too Proud to Beg.' I'm not sure what happened after that. I think we disbanded shortly after.

There used to be a couple of places where bands gathered after gigs. One was Alex's Pie Stand in the City Centre.

We would talk about the gig we'd just come back from, or what gigs we had coming up and just general stuff about gigs, equipment etc.

The other was outside Snow Hill Railway Station. One buddy, sadly no longer with us was a fellow drummer, Kex Gorin. We used to have a saying: 'bags the crust' because we'd buy a steak pie each and because they were so delicious we would by a third one to share and he would always say it. The Americans say 'I called dibs.'

One weekend in the summer, I was playing with The Wellington Kitch Jump Band at The Bull on the Coventry Road. The venue was a popular one with most bands. When we had finished I went over to the bar to say 'Hi' to Robert Plant and he complimented us on the sets we had just done.

I told him that I was going to King Arthur's Court in Gas Street, because I had a ticket to see The Count Basie Band.

After a couple of drinks, I said I was going to phone a cab to get to town, at which point he offered me a lift as he was going into the centre.

So, I gladly accepted, as I didn't drive in those days. He had a Morris Minor convertible that I called the 'Midwife's car.'

Along the way we chatted about gigs and music as in those days most musicians played the same circuits of venues.

So we all compared our experience at the various gigs. As we hit town, I was going to get out and walk to Broad Street, but he said he was going up to Five Ways so he could drop me on Broad Street which was fine as Gas Street was just off there.

I thanked Robert, and went in to the club.

I made it just in time as the band struck up their first number. I very cheekily crept to the front, and ended up, about 2ft away from the man himself, Count Basie. What a night! What a band! Sonny Payne what a great drummer!

If you were in to big band music you couldn't wish for anything better than the Count Basie band. They really knew how to swing.

They played such numbers as 'April in Paris', 'One O' Clock Jump,' 'Swinging the Blues' and many more classics. Brilliant!

I met Robert a couple of more times many years later when I was living in London.

I used to do bit of delivering for two of my dearest friends, Angela and Juliet. They owned a picture framing franchise called the 'Frame Factory' in Belsize Park.

One day I went in and they told me that they had a pop star looking guy come in the other day and he needed some canvasses to be put on frames.

So I asked who he was and they said they weren't sure, but that he had long curly blond hair and looked like a typical rock star.

'There's only one way to find out,' I said. 'Take a look at the name on the receipt.' (Elementary dear Sherlock).

'Plant' was the answer. I then proceeded to explain a bit about Zeppelin. They said he looked a bit different to what they had seen on TV. So I said that's because he didn't come in the shop with his shirt open, and clutching a mic stand perhaps. We had a laugh about it for a while.

'When are these canvasses due for delivery?' I asked.

'They're done, so anytime really'. Angela said.

So I picked these canvasses up, stuck them in the car and off I went with the receipt with the address on. It was just around the corner, a couple of roads away. Off I went and knocked on the door. It was Rob himself who came to the door. 'What the...

What are you doing here?' he said, then he called his other half, who I knew from Birmingham and said, 'Have a look who's here'... she was surprised to see me too.

We spent fifteen to twenty minutes, just catching up. I couldn't stay too long, because I had other deliveries. So hand shakes all round, and I was off to the next call. I love coincidences, don't you?

The second time I bumped in to him was in Upper Street in Islington. He was looking in a shop window that sold Art Deco furnishings, and there were a few clocks in the window. The shop was shut on that particular day.

So I went up to him and said 'Hi' and he asked me if I lived around the area. I said yes, this my manor, so to speak.

I said, 'You know who owns this shop don't you?'

'No,' he says.

It's Chris Farlowe.' I said
So I went on to explain that Chris had a war
memorabilia shop before this one and that I
occasionally bump into him from time to time as he
lives in Islington. With that we went to a greasy spoon
cafe in Cross Street and had a good old natter about the
old days in Brum. He asked me what I was up to
nowadays, and we just talked generally about our ages
and stuff and after a couple of rounds of tea we left the
cafe.
He jumped in a bright red sports car and I jumped on a
big red bus. 'That's Showbiz,' as they say.

## CLUBS IN BIRMINGHAM

Another club I worked in was The Opposite Lock. It
was run by Martin Hone, who happened to be a
Formula One racing fanatic, hence the name of the club
(a motoring term for turning the wheel). There were
two floors: downstairs was a bar and a small stage,
which was just big enough to accommodate a trio.
That's where I played congas with Graham Tyson on a
Hammond organ with bass foot pedals, and Keith
Seeley, drums.
We would play the earlier part of the evening and then
later, around 11.30 we would hand over to the DJ,
Frankie Lee.

Meanwhile upstairs, in Martin's Bar, there was another
trio. They were: Johnny Andrews piano, Tubby Dunn,
bass guitar, and my old mate Malcolm Priddy, on
drums. They were more jazz inclined - all great
musicians.
Closing time was 2am, and about ten or fifteen minutes
after 2am, the DJ was instructed to put this particular
record on. It was a soundtrack of a real Formula One
race, and it was played loud, just a roaring of cars
engines revving etc. Most of the regulars soon got the

hint, and they went and got their coats from the cloakroom.

It was the most unique way to clear a club at closing time that I've ever known.

I watched some great acts there at the club, performers such as: The Peddlers.

Just a few short lines about The Peddlers. They were a class act consisting of: Roy Phillips Hammond organ /vocals, Tab Martin on bass guitar and Trevor Morais on drums. Superb musicians and very entertaining to watch. They played Jazz and Blues in their own unique way. Their repertoire included couple of Jon Hendrix songs. Jon Hendrix (of Lambert, Hendrix and Ross), and many more...

It was in this very place much later that I first heard the news about John Lennon's death. I, like everyone else, was totally stunned!


There were a couple more clubs that I used to frequent and also played at. One was 'The Elbow Room' in Aston, which believe it or not, is still there. This is where I last saw Ozzy.

I walked in one night and he was sitting on the side with Sharon, and as soon as he saw me, he leapt out of his seat, and came over and picked me up right off the ground, and invited me to join them. I have known Sharon for ages, because her father Don Arden was our manager in Wizzard.

She used to come on the road with us and sometimes with her brother David.

Back to the Elbow Room, it had a lovely atmosphere; I used to love playing there. Stevie Winwood used to come in occasionally and the rest of 'Traffic' as well. In fact it was here that 'Traffic' got together for the first time.

I remember playing there one night when John Bonham ended up on my kit and I sat beside him and passed him drinks in between numbers.

Big Albert, who was running it at the time, was also managing Black Sabbath. He used to go to school with Tony Iommi the guitarist they remained close friends. There used to be jam sessions on a regular basis; the club had a relaxing atmosphere. Great club!

There was also The Rum Runner on Broad Street. This is where 'Big Albert' was the head doorman before he owned the 'Elbow Room'.
I spent many a Saturday night in that place.
Occasionally, usually on Saturday nights, there would inevitably be a couple of undesirables who would cause trouble and Albert would sweep into action. He was subtle and quick. Before you knew it, the troublemakers were being marched outside.
Job done!!
I was there on a regular basis. Again loads of musicians played and drank in there.
One of the first 'house' bands, playing the cover versions of the day, became 'Magnum' featuring Bob Catley and Tony Clarkin.
They have since become legends and they've released several albums; they have a huge following.
They left the club in 1975 to play their own material of melodic rock. Occasionally other live acts played there as well, such bands as Quill and Jigsaw.
Regular late night clientele were Black Sabbath, Roy Wood, Bandylegs, Quartz and other notable Birmingham bands calling in after local gigs. The decor was simple - a bar in the middle and seating to the sides. On one side the seating consisted of huge barrels, which seated four with a table in between the seats. They were quite cosy, especially when you were with a young lady.

Mick Walker who also worked at the Rum Runner was the only guy I know who did three jobs at once. He was a bouncer, musician and comedian. He'd be on stage playing his bass then if a fight broke out he would stop playing. The rest of the band played on and he would sort out the trouble alongside 'Albert' by throwing the guys out of the front door then come back in and carry on playing. He was also very funny. At the end of the night when the band had finished he would stand on stage and tell gags. He was a natural comedian and when the time came to get people out, he would say something like, 'All right. We've had your money now piss off!'

Everybody knew him and knew he was just joking, but it worked and they would all get their coats from the cloakroom and leave.

Mick was originally with a band called The Redcaps along with his brother Dave; they had a couple of minor hits.

Dave later joined the Savoy Brown Blues Band, Fleetwood Mac, and a few more bands. They were great blue's vocalists.

Mick is still on the circuit as an after dinner speaker, stand-up comedian and he also does a bit of playing still.

One night I was in Abigail's another one of Eddie Fewtrell's clubs. The star act that week was Buddy Greco. He was known more for his singing but he was also a great pianist too. In fact he played piano for the Benny Goodman band in the forties. He had success with the old standard 'The Lady is a Tramp.'

As he was on all week I saw him again the following night as well, only this time there was a bonus because that was the night that Jack Jones came in to see him. Jack was on at another venue in town called The Big Night Out and as he finished there earlier than Buddy he came in and the inevitable happened- he got up and sang with him. You would have to pay good money to see that.

The next night I was in again and sure enough Jack came in again. He was with his sound engineer and his manager. Someone introduced me to him and I was invited to sit at his table. We chatted about his show and just general chitchat. Then Jack asked me if I had seen his show. I said no I hadn't because it was sold out for the whole week.

'Come tomorrow night as my guest,' he said, and his sound engineer said 'You can stand by my sound desk, no problem.' So the sound guy arranged to meet me in the foyer half an hour before the start of the show and he walked me in. The sound guy told me that they were going to be recording that night's performance.

Well! As expected, Jack was terrific. He has an incredible voice. He went through some old standards that are associated with him like: 'Girl Talk', 'Wives and Lovers' and one of my favourite ballads 'Here's that Rainy Day.'

After the show I went to Abigail's and a little while later Jack and his entourage came in and there were drinks all round, then even more drinks. The one thing that puzzled me was that Jack smoked; with such an amazing voice you would have thought that he was a non-smoker. We were there until way after the club officially closed as guests of Eddie the owner. Eventually we all made a move to go, we said our goodbyes, I thanked them for the night and left. As it was in the summer it was daylight outside.

It was that same summer by way of contrast from the above. I went to see Black Sabbath at the Town Hall. First of all, during the gig, I noticed that I was the only person actually sitting down - the rest of the punters were on their feet playing air guitar and head banging. Geyser's bass was actually vibrating my seat, and I was up in the circle!, that should give you a rough idea of the decibel levels. I did not envy Bill Ward at all. The energy and stamina needed to play drums in that way was something I could not see myself doing. I am not putting anyone down, I mean, they're all old mates from way back. They went down a storm and got the crowd into a frenzy. After the gig I went backstage and they all greeted me. After they all changed and relaxed a bit we all went to the Elbow Room, which was their usual haunt. The Elbow Room is in Newtown, which is just down the road from Aston, where they all came from. It was somewhere near 4am and that's when we all went up to the city centre and into a curry house. The manager welcomed us in and showed us to a table. Only in Birmingham! I mean where else can you go for a curry at 4 in the morning? We were there for a little over an hour, then Tony Iommi gave me lift. I was living in Nechells at the time.

The nice thing about all of the Birmingham musicians was that between us there were no airs and graces. We all knew each other from the days when we all started out so we were all like a family.

## GHOST

The band Ghost was a little different from most of the other bands that I'd been involved with in as much as, we only did original material with lots of close harmony vocals. The subject matter was a bit on the dark side for me, mostly about witches and warlocks. Having said that Shirley Kent was and still is a fabulous vocalist and songwriter and her songs were gentle and poignant. She reminds me a little of Janice Ian – such a sweet voice.

All the guys were very strong vocal wise. Paul Eastment had a raunchy, gravelly voice and he was also a mean blues guitarist. Terry Guy (keyboards/vocals) did most of the high falsetto stuff.

And last but not least… Danny McGuire (bass/vocals). Great voice and very versatile; he later started doing gigs on his own on guitar and vocals.

We did an album called 'When You're Dead,' which I believe has now become a collector's item.

I remember seeing it in a collector's magazine for a
£100.

I'm still in touch with Paul from time to time.

One of the venues we played at was the famous
Liverpool Cavern which, at the time was quite exciting
knowing that it was such a prestigious venue. In actual
fact the place smelt a bit with a mixture of
condensation, dampness from the walls, body heat, etc.
The place used to get extremely packed. I remember I
did a drum solo and when I finished I was feeling faint
with the heat. The condensation from the low ceiling
was dripping on my drums but having said that it was a
good crowd and we were well received.

I played it once more with another band - sorry can't
remember the name.

At another time I played it with the Wellington Kitch
Band but this was the New Cavern, which was across
the road and it wasn't the same atmosphere at all.

## MONGREL

As Carl Wayne was no longer with The Move - he was
doing more solo work. A few of us musicians got
together to form a backing band for him.

The line up was: Roger Hill guitar, Rick Price bass
guitar, Bob Brady, keyboard/vocals, Keith Smart
drums, and yours truly congas/percussion.

We rehearsed for a few weeks at The Cedar Club, but
after a while Carl started getting more session work and
offers of singer/compere work so he left the band.

We all wished him well and all parted as friends.

As we had a ready-made band, instead of breaking up,
we decided to carry on. Around this time Bob Brady
had penned a good few songs so we rehearsed those
and Rick used to do a couple of songs, as did Roger and

between us we had enough material for a couple of decent sets.

Oh! And that was the first time I ever sang in public. I used to sing a song called 'Theme From an Imaginary Western' - I believe it was a Jack Bruce song and Leslie West of Mountain did it also.

Around 1970 we went into Air Studios on Oxford Circus. George Martin owned it. We recorded an album called 'Get Your Teeth Into This,' which was produced by Jon Miller, but we all pitched in our ideas especially Bob Brady, as most of the tracks were his compositions.

We carried on gigging in and around Brum for a while. One night we played at The Belfry now known more for its golf course.

We didn't know that Roy Wood was in the audience until he came backstage to say 'hi' to Rick.

Rick had been in The Move (the second version). They have had a few personnel changes during the years.

After Roy left, Rick told us that he had arranged to see Roy at his house to have a chat.

It later transpired that Roy was thinking of leaving ELO. Not sure why exactly but one can only assume that there may have been artistic differences between him and Jeff Lynne, after all, they were both talented songwriters/ producers plus multi instrumentalists.

So a meeting was set up at Gothersley Hall (Roy's house) and a few of us went.

He then told us that he was thinking of starting another band and he wanted to know if we would be interested in coming in on it. He already had Hugh McDowell (cello), Bill Hunt (keyboards) from ELO on board. So he was interested in Keith, drums, Rick, bass and me, congas.

We were torn between our loyalty to Mongrel or this new venture with Roy.

When we left Roy's we talked it over amongst ourselves and it was difficult because we didn't want to let the rest of the guys down, but we were tempted with the offer because Roy was a step up.

After much deliberation we decided to go for it. I made a small stipulation regarding my role in the band, and that was, that I didn't want to play just percussion. Without any hesitation Roy said, 'We'll have two drummers then.' It was that simple! and that was how Wizzard was born.

## WIZZARD

Roy had some financial backing from his record label Harvest, to spend on gear.

Because we had two drummers (quite a few bands had two drummers in those days) we were sponsored by Beverly Drums.

So Keith and myself were given a red Beverly double kit each, which consisted of: two bass drums, two floor tom-toms, the usual two nest tom- toms, five cymbals, a hi hat, plus all the stands.

Off we went on this new venture.

As well as Hugh McDowell and Bill Hunt, there were another couple of cellists and of course Mike Burney and Nick Pentelow on various saxes.

I had known Nick from earlier when we both used to frequent a Community Centre in Cannon Hill Park. Bob Johnson who is better known nowadays as Bob Carolgees, with Spit the Dog ran the Centre at that time.

I used to spend a lot of time there. I got involved in helping backstage and used the practice rooms.

All in all we were now an eleven piece.

We rehearsed for around a month or so in Roy's garage, which was rather large. It had to be in order to accommodate all of us.

Then the first gig was at none other than Wembley Stadium at the 1972 Rock 'n' Roll Festival.
It started around midday and went on through to around 11pm. The headlining acts were: Bill Haley, Chuck Berry, Little Richard, Jerry Lee Lewis and Bo Diddley, so we were in good company.

The stadium was packed with about 85 to 90 thousand people, mostly bikers.
They put a tarpaulin on the actual pitch because that way they could get more in than a football match.
We went to have a look just as it started. I can't remember who was on at the time, but I got the shock of my life as we were in the wings so to speak. The stage was built across one of the tunnels where the players normally come out and it seemed massive... we stayed a short while then went back to our hotel.
After a short rest, a shower and a bite to eat we made our way back to the Festival.
The band immediately before us were pelted with beer cans.

As the time got nearer to going on I started getting the old butterflies in the stomach.
When we eventually went on, the first thing I did was to higher my cymbal stands and tilt the cymbals to act as shields should we get the same reception.
Fortunately we didn't, so I relaxed a bit more.
After about 3 or 4 numbers, I used to come off my kit and walk to the front of the stage where my congas were set up.
I used them on a song called 'Forever' (from Roy's own solo album).
Later on in the set both Keith and I used to do a solo each then I used to leave my kit again and do a solo on the congas. It's hard to explain the buzz you get as you connect with a big crowd like that. Good feeling!

All in all, the gig went well considering that the fold-back on stage wasn't that great and it was the very first gig.

A few days later we went into the studios to record an album with Bo Diddley. It was aptly called 'Bo Diddley, 'The London Sessions'. Not a very imaginative title, but it had nothing to do with us. We were just playing on it.

Shortly after that we went into EMI, Abbey Road studios and cut our first single 'Ballpark Incident.' The first thing that strikes you as you walk in to the actual studio is the size. It was like an airplane hangar. I noticed The Beatles drum-kit tucked away in one corner. Here's a little interesting fact about that particular recording.
In those days we used to remove the front skin off the bass drums and pack some blankets to muffle the sound and the engineer would put a microphone inside.
Well, so as not to lose all the metal fittings that held the skin on I had put them in a tom-tom case.
As I just finished doing that and picked the case up to move it, Roy happened to be in earshot, and he said, "We'll use that."

I had no idea what he was talking about. He was referring to the noise that the case made with the fittings inside.
Sure enough that sound was used in the intro. I would pick it up and bang it onto an empty tom-tom case to achieve the initial sound then Roy and the engineer would add a few tweaks ... reverb, flanger effect, etc. until we got the sound you can hear on the finished recording. All clever stuff!
Each one of us wrote a 'B'side to all our hits.
Mine was called 'Dream of Unwin.' It was an instrumental and I played piano.

The title is a play on words. There's a tune called 'Dream of Olwen,' an orchestral piece, and mine was Unwin named after Professor Stanley Unwin. Some people will remember him - a very funny guy who had his own language. He was always on some show or other on TV and radio.

The 'A' side was 'Rock n Roll Winter.'

The 'B' side to our first single 'Ballpark Incident,' was written by Bill Hunt and called 'The Carlsberg Special' ( Pianos demolished phone*********).

Let me explain the title...

Bill Hunt was the first keyboard player in Wizzard and on stage (at open air gigs mainly) he used to physically demolish an old piano - I mean take it apart, bit by bit and throw it into the pit in front of the stage where there was a barrier for the press. I have to say that he is a very accomplished musician on keyboards and French horn and the piano wrecking was just a bit of fun. The road crew had acquired a couple of old pianos at some of the gigs, and that's how it started. So to get back to the title...we decided to put the 'pianos demolished' bit and his real landline number just for a laugh. Well of course he was inundated with calls from fans asking all sort of questions.

It's a wonder it didn't wreck his marriage. He reckoned the phone was ringing constantly so he was forced to change it in the end. The 'Carlsberg' bit came about from the fact that when in a studio recording session we used to have a crate or two of Carlsberg Special Brew which had just come out at the time, as well as some spirits, wine etc. for medicinal purpose only, you understand!

Well!! When we had a presentation afternoon for the single and collected our silver discs a representative from Carlsberg brewery presented us with a couple of crates of the stuff.

The presentation was held at The Magic Circle Club
Headquarters in London.
The music press was invited as were a couple of
magazines.
All in all it was a nice afternoon.

## MARC BOLAN

Roy Wood and I used to go to a couple of clubs now
and again. One night we went to Abigail's and when
we had been there a little while Marc Bolan came in.
T Rex had been playing at the Town Hall.
He came and joined our table. We chatted awhile
mainly about their gig, and quite a few drinks later we
drove him to the Holiday Inn near Broad Street. We
would have stayed for a drink but we had to be up early
the next morning. We were just about to leave but he
wouldn't let us leave until Roy picked a pair of shoes
from a huge selection to take home as a present, so Roy
did just that and we left.

There's too much that happened over the three year
lifespan of Wizzard to cram into these pages so here's a
condensed version. As I never kept a diary it's all down
to memory, I'm afraid.

We played most major venues up and down the country
and a few open-air festivals such as Reading, Buxton
and quite a few on the continent, Holland, Germany,
Finland, Ah!... In Finland we played an open-air
festival in Torku.
Now when I say played that's not entirely true. Let me
explain ... we were halfway through a Scandinavian
tour and when we finished Sweden, we flew to Torku
but our roadies with our gear were obviously coming
by road. Well I'm not sure what happened exactly, but
we got to the town of Torku and checked in to our
hotel. We then had a call from our roadies saying that

they were having some kind of problem with the truck, so as a precaution, someone suggested to hire us some gear locally - a back line for Roy and Rick, a couple of drum kits for Keith and myself.

On this gig we were on with Status Quo. We'd met them in the foyer of the hotel where we were all staying. Later on in the afternoon we went to the gig in a coach, which was to be our dressing room as well. The 'Quo' made their own way there, as they weren't on until much later.

So we got there with a couple of hours to spare. We stayed on the coach as this was our dressing room and all our stage clothes were in it.

So now it was time to go on, so off we went towards the stage, we waited at the side for the signal from whoever was in charge and we walked on before Roy as usual. I sat at my kit, sorry not my kit, but the hired kit, it obviously didn't feel the same, but we had to make do.

On came Roy; he plugged in his guitar and off we went. I think we started with 'Ballpark Incident.' That's when it started to go pear shaped! All the way through the song we could see Roy getting more agitated by the minute. He wasn't getting the same sound as with his own gear and about three quarters of the way through the song he came over to his amplifiers stack (which incidentally was about two feet away from my left ear) and he suddenly kicked the whole lot over, then he unplugged his guitar and stormed off stage…Well, we carried on to the end of the song then we just glanced at each other and walked off the stage too.

We joined Roy in the coach. He was still fuming, totally disgusted with the cheap equipment that they had hired for us. We told the driver of the coach to take us back to our hotel. It was easier said than done, because he had to try and manoeuvre the coach through the crowd that had gathered around it and they were pissed off with us and banging on the side of the coach as it drove slowly through them.

With lots of luck, we eventually managed to get through and headed back to the hotel. On arrival at the hotel, we went and dumped our clothes and bags in our rooms and did what any bunch of decent chaps would do in our position - hit the bar and indulged in the partaking of a few libations.

After a couple of hours, Francis and the rest of Quo came into the bar and asked us what happened. Well, we weren't sure and we were now at the stage where we couldn't care less. 'Have a drink fellas,' we told them, and that folks…was my experience of Finland.

The Germany gig was in an amphitheatre in Frankfurt. We were on with Deep Purple, Status Quo and a couple of local bands. From what I can recall, we received a good reception from the crowd.

We had our own gear this time so it went a bit smoother than Finland.

## TOP OF THE POPS

Years ago when I was just starting out, I used to do a regular Thursday night in a pub not far from where I lived in Nechells. The pub was The Railway in Curzon Street.

It was just John Killigrew on piano /vocals and myself on kit. We would play a whole assortment of covers: rock, country and standards. The night was called (here's a word for the over forties) a 'Free and Easy' night. It meant that in the second half of the night we would invite singers up to sing the same bloody song week after week.

Anyway, there was a television set on the stage and it would be on while I set my kit up. Then we would have to wait till Top of the Pops finished before we would make a start.

I used to wonder what it would be like to be on that programme as it always looked like fun.

We played that place for a quite some time.

John and I were the first live musicians they had at that pub.

A few years later The Railway became a well-known music venue - the place to be seen and heard.

Sadly it closed down recently as did most of the great venues in and around Brum.


Moving on to the Top of the Pops show.

The show was recorded at 7.30 pm and they let the audience in at 7pm. We had to be there at 11am for rehearsal and we'd have to hang about for more rehearsals, this time for the cameras.

Sometimes if we were lucky, they would give us a round- about time that they needed us, which gave us some time to leave the building and nip down to Shepherds Bush.

It all depended on how many live acts were on that particular episode. But otherwise we would stay in the dressing room or go the canteen. I have to say, the food was quite good for a works canteen.

When we had the second rehearsal we would have our costumes on.

On one occasion Roy, for some reason only known to him, decided that it would be a good idea to put Keith, the other drummer and myself in ballerina tutus

So Rick, the bass player took us to Camden to Bermans the theatrical costumers to get these tutus. It took a considerable amount of scotch to get me to actually wear the damn thing I can tell you.

I remember that as we were on the set before going on the stage I was having a conversation with Clem Cattini, one of the top session drummers in the UK. It was weird because it wasn't until I was well into the chat that I happened to look down and realised I was standing there with this bloody skirt on. We knew that bands used to mime on the show, so we didn't try to hide it. For instance, on the occasion with the tutu, Keith and I were nowhere near a drum kit - we were each twirling a double bass. Still we had fun.

One Christmas episode we were on with Slade and Keith and I thought it would be a bit of fun to get a couple of theatrical custard pies and while Noddy was singing their Christmas hit, we went on stage and let him have it in the face. The only reason we did it is because we were good buddies with them and we knew that Noddy would take it as a joke and a bit of fun.

We also had some of our road crew dressed up in gorilla suits. They were sweating their bits off under those hot lights.

Still, I think they secretly enjoyed it.

The best bit was when the show finished and we would adjourn to the bar on the fourth floor. It was a members only bar so we would have to get someone to sign us in which was silly when you've been there all day. You would think you wouldn't have to do that just to get a drink.

Sometimes we used to bribe the guy at the desk in the entrance to the bar with a pint of Guinness.

There were a couple of occasions where we'd go in and about an hour later realise that we'd forgotten to take his pint, but he would deny all knowledge of it if his boss happened to be there, which was not that often thank God.

I use to love it when we were on with Abba. The girls were even better looking in person, so to speak.

I remember Cliff was on once and he sang live with the BBC orchestra. There was no miming for him.

All in all we did Top of the Pops on a regular basis while the singles were in the charts.

Each time with a sillier 'get up' than the last time.

But on the whole, it was fun.

# THE USA

The American Tour was set up for around 5 weeks.
At the time we were with the Warner Bros label.
When we arrived at J.F.K, we were met by a couple of
executives and when we were through picking up our
luggage, they walked us through to two black shining
limos.
We were driven to our hotel, across the road from The
Radio City building. We were all a little excited, seeing
New York for the first time but of course Roy and Rick
had been to the states before with The Move, so they
were a little less in awe of the place.
To think I was just down the road from the famous
Carnegie Hall where so many great names had
appeared,
We just mooched around for a few hours then took a
walk down to Times Square.
I remember some woman came up to us and handed me
a small posy of flowers. That's nice I thought, so this is
what New York is like, until she asked me for 5 dollars
for the flowers.
So she got them back straight away!
Later on that night I was feeling a little peckish so I
asked for a ham sandwich. After about twenty minutes
there came a knock on my door. It was the night porter
with my ham sandwich. Now I'm not tight fisted, I just
genuinely hadn't quite grasped the concept of the UK
and US dollar conversion, so I gave the guy, what I
thought was a generous tip. Obviously not, because he
looked at me and said, 'Two lousy dollars? I had to go
across the *@%$ street to get this damn sandwich...'so
I gave him another couple of dollars. Some people
would have told him to go and...(you can fill this in
yourself). That's one hell of a room service, I thought.
Our first gig was in New Jersey at a venue called The
Joint in the Woods. It was just that - a large shack in
the middle of this thicket, a kind of dirt road, leading to

a car park and the building a bit like a barn. Once you got inside it was absolutely huge. We went down quite well considering we weren't known over there. Roy had a bit of a following, because of the time he was there with The Move, but Wizzard was something new.

Obviously I can't remember the whole of the five weeks, but I'll highlight a couple of the more interesting times.

At this time we were an eleven-piece band.
We ran into a few problems because of that.
For instance:
The Denver gig never happened because the stage apparently wasn't big enough. So we spent four days there without playing a note.
The Trio that played in the lounge of the Holiday Inn where we were staying were somewhat baffled by all this. 'Aren't you guys supposed to be playing tonight?'... They said this every night.
There wasn't much we the musicians could do so we left it up to the road crew, at which point our Manager Don Arden turned up (he was already in the States on business) so we left it up to him to sort it all out with the local promoter.
It was blazing hot and the outdoor pool at the Holiday Inn was ideal for cooling down.
I jumped in with all my clothes on one time, which isn't bad, considering I don't swim a stroke.

Mike Burney is a steam-train enthusiast, and he knew that there was a train called `Big Boy' at the Transport Museum here in Denver so we paid it a visit.
Sure enough there it was, this massive train plus some amazing old cars. They had: Buicks, Chevrolets, Lincolns, and Duesenbergs. Fabulous! I am not a connoisseur of cars by any means but I liked the shape of American cars of the 50's.

I remember my brother Johnny used to drive a taxi back home in Malta and in those days there were a lot of American cars on the Island. He used to drive a Buick or sometimes a Pontiac.

They have a beautiful shape and all that chrome just enhances the design.

Atlanta: The venue was a thousand-odd seater and from what I remember the gig was not bad - we only had to do a short set.

The following morning our tour manager Bernie with his early-morning call woke us up, 'Come on you bunch of b--------ds! Let's burn some rubber! We've got a plane to catch.'

When we arrived at the airport still pissed from the night before, I remember Mike was having problems with his suitcase; he couldn't close it. There were a few bits of clothing hanging out, so a few of us tried to help him. There we were on the pavement, struggling with the suitcase when this Mercedes pulls up, and the driver leant out of the window and asked if we were a band. So I went over to talk to him and as I talked to him, I noticed that sitting in the back was Joe Frazier, the boxer. So I told them the name of the band and I told Joe that he knew our Manager, Don Arden, to which he replied, 'Ask him when is he gonna set up another U.K tour for me.'

A few years previously Joe came to the UK to do a tour as a soul singer, which Don promoted.

Phoenix: was hot, very hot, and this was September. We stayed at a motel, with an outdoor pool, probably the best place we'd stayed in on the whole tour.

The gig was a huge circular building, with a revolving stage. I remember us going there the night before our gig to see Joe Jackson. The place was packed solid and there was also a prominent smell of smoke coming from inside the place, and it certainly wasn't Woodbines.

We hired a couple of buggies, and drove off to the desert, which was just a few miles away from the motel. It was real cowboy country complete with ten - foot cacti.

A bit further on up the road we came to a little town, which was strictly a tourist trap and was just like a Western-film set with a saloon with swinging doors and all.

There was a store there that sold boots, shirts, saddles, hats, and all sorts of leather goods.

I bought a cowboy shirt from there. It had flowers embroidered near the shoulders. I loved that shirt. Every time I wore it I swear I could hear Hank Williams singing 'Your Cheating Heart.'

Oh yes! I nearly forgot, this place was called Rawhide...not surprising really.

As you entered the gates to this pretend town there was a bunch of mechanical cowboys sitting around a pretend fire. The scene was obviously based on the farting scene in Mel Brook's 'Blazing Saddles' but I can't quite recall whether there were sound effects though.

I don't remember much about Philadelphia; except that it was the first time I'd seen an actual ghetto complete with those front-door stoops that you see in TV cop shows.

Somewhere around the middle of the tour we went to Canada for a one-night stand in Toronto. The venue was the Ryerson University Theatre.

It turned out to be a bit of a let down.

You see, there was a radio station on the campus and we were picking it up on our speakers, so it was like two bands trying to play at once. It was impossible to carry on.

So we ended the set after half an hour.

Well, I can tell you we weren't thrilled with the gig and Roy was fuming, but eventually he calmed down and then someone from the university offered to take us for a Chinese meal and off we went.

As it was only one night, all I saw of Toronto was the gig and yet another Holiday Inn, plus a really good Chinese restaurant on Young Street.

In Detroit we supported Kiss. The hotel was right across the street from the venue, which was huge. From the hotel we watched as the punters started queuing. The queue went right around the building.

We didn't kid ourselves - they were there for their idols Kiss. We were well received considering.

Kiss is a very heavy metal band, they all wear black and white makeup. After we finished, most of us hung around to watch their set. Not exactly my kind of music but they went down extremely well.

After the whole thing finished there was a party at the hotel...

It went on till at least 5am.

The guys from Kiss were really friendly and I as I chatted to the drummer, I was a little surprised to find that he was into big band Jazz.

Between the two bands we drank the hotel bar out of Tequila. They only had two bottles then they had to send out for some more.

We had a week or so in LA where we did two TV shows. One was 'Don Kirshner's Rock Concert.' This show was live from Santa Monica Civic Hall and we were on the bill with 'Sparks'.

The other TV show was filmed in Burbank Studios where we used the same stage that they used to film 'The Dean Martin Show.' I remember it was like a plane hangar, with Dean's silhouette stencilled on the huge doors.

We were on with Kiki Dee, who performed her hit at that time, 'I've Got The Music In Me', which she sang live. It was very impressive, since it was early in the morning.

The hotel we stayed at was on Sunset Strip. It was The Hyatt House Hotel, nicknamed by bands as the 'Riot House.' The swimming pool was on the roof. We spent quite a bit of time there during the day, trying to get a bit of colour so we can blend in with the other bronzed bodies there.

Right across the street from the hotel was Dino's Lodge which was a restaurant and nightclub, owned by none other than D M himself.

The address of the Lounge was 79 Sunset Strip, and right next door was the fictional address of the Private Eye Agency in the TV show, '77 Sunset Strip.'

They filmed the opening of the show right there (the rest of the show was filmed on the Warner Bros Studios Lot).

Who can forget names like Efrem Zimbalist Jnr, Roger Smith and Ed 'Kookie' Burns?

I seem to remember it was in black and white, so that dates it a bit I guess.

We had quite a bit of time to ourselves, while in LA, to seek out any jazz on anywhere. Mike Burney noticed that there was a band called Super Sax playing for 3 nights in a place called Donte's on Lankersham Boulevard.

I personally had never heard of the band. The band's repertoire consists of Charlie Parker tunes, pieces like: 'Scrapple from the Apple' 'Lover Man' 'Ornithology,' etc.

Med Flory, a saxophonist and also a bit-part actor in movies - westerns, led the band.

We ended up going there every night, and got talking with the guys. By the third night we were like old buddies.

They used to dedicate a couple of pieces. Here's one for the guys from the UK,' they used to say.

The drummer was none other than Jake Hanna, an old hero of mine he was with Woody Herman for many years; great guy, great drummer.

While we were there we met a lovely tall young lady who introduced herself as Dana Kenton. She was only the daughter of the brilliant bandleader Stan Kenton wasn't she! When we were about to leave at the end of the night she asked if we wanted to go to another jazz club.

No prize for guessing our reply! We caught a cab and she told the driver The Baked Potato and off we went. The club was small and intimate, no entry fee as long as you purchased a couple of beers. There were a bunch of musicians just setting up and soon after they started playing some nice cool jazz. Within a few minutes the place started filling up and musicians came in carrying their respective instrument cases, which they duly opened, and before you knew it they joined in. Great atmosphere. Most of the musicians knew Dana...well who didn't know Stan Kenton, pianist, composer and bandleader? His most well known tune was 'Peanut Vendor.'

While still in Hollywood we met a guy who worked at Capitol Records and Mike Burney mentioned a Nat King Cole album that was on the Capitol label, and right away the guy invited us to go to the Capitol Building in the morning and he'd see what he could do. So the next day we went round there to the famous Capitol Tower on Hollywood and Vine.

As we walked in we stood there in the foyer with our mouths open. You've never seen so many silver, gold and platinum discs.

All of the walls were plastered with discs of Sinatra, Dean Martin, Nat King Cole, Beach Boys, Beatles and many more

The guy came down to greet us, and he apologised that he only found a couple of the Nat King Cole albums and as there were quite a few of us he asked for an address and said he would send us one each. We all thought it might be an excuse just to get rid of us. Anyway I gave him my address and true to his word within a few days of us getting back to the UK they arrived at my door.

One night we went to a club on Hermosa Beach called The Lighthouse. It was quite well known as a jazz venue.

I actually have a couple of performances recorded there. As we went in we could hear this wonderful marimba sound.

For those who are not familiar with the instrument, it's a wooden vibraphone (xylophone), and playing it was none other than the amazing Bobby Hutcherson.

We stayed there until closing time. Hutcherson is one of my favourite vibes players along side Milt Jackson, Gary Burton and, of course the one and only Lionel Hampton.

Just before we were getting ready to go home one of the guys that took us there introduced us to this other guy.

Now, this guy was a scientist, poet and a philosopher. He also did a laser show. He invited all of us to his place for a nightcap.

As we were with the guy who introduced us to him, we felt obliged to go. This guy lived in what I can only describe as a disused warehouse. The whole place was littered with dismantled TV sets, radio sets, and an array of electrical gadgets and gizmos. In one corner amongst all this stuff was his single bed. Then he showed us this small piece of plastic with a photo of a skull, which was imbedded within this plastic. As you moved this plastic around the skull became 3D. It was a hologram. Now I know it doesn't sound a big deal nowadays but in those days there weren't that many holograms about and in fact that was the first time any of us had seen one.

Meeting this guy was a bit like early cavemen meeting Einstein. He really blew our minds with the things he was coming out with. For instance, he had a theory that in the future, scientists would be able to pick up sounds from a wall, window pane, or any object and they would hear conversations that were spoken near that wall...etc.

I know that sounds weird, but only recently I heard or read that very same thing. This guy was way ahead. That was one of the highlights of the whole tour.

## CABARET

Before we finally flew home, we went back to New York. We played at the Academy of Music, and did two shows, one about 6 pm and the other around 10 pm, if I remember right.

Later our tour manager Bernie took Bob Brady and myself to a nightclub; the club was called 'Reno Sweeney's'.

After about half an hour of being there, this beautiful girl came in and she looked straight in our direction and gave us a huge smile as she came towards us.

Now!! We've all seen the scenario where one person walks towards another with arms outstretched and as they get really close you discover that they're really going for the person behind. Well!! That's exactly what happened with her - she was smiling at Andy Warhol who was on a table behind ours. We later had a bit of a laugh about it. I remember Bernie saying to us, 'In your dreams, matey.'

A little while later the house band came on and they were absolutely brilliant. They played a few instrumentals a mixture of jazz, funk and soul.
They did a short set for about 20 minutes then they introduced four singers, two guys and two women, all dressed really smart; the guys wore tuxedos. They were a close harmony group, really slick and polished.
They were Manhattan Transfer.
I remember Bob and I went backstage afterwards and met them and we told them how much we enjoyed their show and that they should come over to the UK.
They said that they wanted to do Europe sometime, but at the moment they were really busy with quite a few commitments. We wished them well and left.
When we got downstairs to go out, we went past this little recess-like booth and we heard this English accent. It turned out to be Peter Cook of Pete 'n' Dud fame.
So we got talking as you do and he told us that he and Dudley Moore were appearing on Broadway with their show 'Beyond the Fringe'. We asked him how it was doing and he said that they were getting good houses, but at times he missed certain things from back home in the UK.
We told him it was a pity that we were not there a bit longer because we'd have loved to come and see them.
We chatted for a bit then it was chucking out time so we all went outside. I remember it was raining;
I'd had a few drinks throughout the evening so I was pretty jolly, and suddenly I turned into Gene Kelly and started doing the routine right there on the pavement, while Bob and the others tried to hail a cab. This seemed to amuse Peter as he watched me.
Then I finished with a jump into an empty dustbin and he was pissing himself laughing at me.

Just after, as I was getting myself together, a cab pulled up and Peter got in and we said our goodbyes and off he went.

We got our cab a few minutes later.

I was absolutely soaked and knackered but it was worth it. What a night!

Altogether we were in the States for five to six weeks.

## BACK IN THE UK

There was a little incident regarding a Range Rover, incoming tide and sand. Let me explain...

It was our second attempt to travel up to Cardiff for a gig at the university. Our first attempt failed because of bad weather and we were going to hire two helicopters to take us up there so we went to this manor in the country. I think it had something to do with the Cadbury's family (sorry to be so vague but hey it has been a long time ago).

I remember seeing the two helicopters on this massive lawn at the back of the house.

We waited while the pilots checked and checked again on the weather situation.

As it got later and later the weather deteriorated so we were forced to call it a day.

So that was the first attempt.

The second attempt featured Roy's Range Rover and a hired car.

We were on our way to Cardiff from our previous night's gig and we decided to stop off at Weston Super Mare, and as you do, we drove onto the beach.

I was in the Range Rover along with two others plus Roy who was driving. Rick was driving the hired car and once on the beach the hired car stopped back while The Range Rover carried on going further towards the sea.

Now, because it had a four wheel drive system we all thought that we would have no problem should we get a bit stuck in the sand ... Wrong!

We did get stuck and Roy tried and tried to get out of the sand but to no avail.

Now, it starts to drizzle and the tide is inching its way inland. Oh! And also the daylight is fading.

Meanwhile the guys in the other car had gone to get help and they came back after what seemed ages, with a truck from a local garage. It had a winch on the back, so they unrolled this cable to try and hook it up to the tow bar on the Range Rover, but it was a good ten or twelve feet too short.

They wouldn't bring the truck any closer in case they got stuck as well.

Now it was really dark, the tide was even closer and it was still drizzling. Eventually the police turned up. They parked on the pavement and they put on this really powerful searchlight and shone it on us in the Range Rover. A couple of them came on foot towards us and told us that the only thing we could do was to empty the car and abandon it. By this time it was well and truly stuck, so we had no option but to comply.

We made a few journeys to the other car with guitars, bags, clothes etc. and bid a fond farewell to the vehicle.

We weren't all going to fit in the hired car so we called a local cab. The cab driver must have thought it was Christmas when we told him to take us to Birmingham. It was an expensive fare but at least the driver was happy.

## BACK IN THE UK: MEETING FRED

When we returned from the States, we had a few days to ourselves.

Then, sometime later we went into De Lane Lea Studios, in Wembley.

De Lane Lea Studios is a recording studios currently based in Dean Street Soho, London, but when we were recording it was in Engineers way in Wembley, adjacent to the old Wembley Stadium.

Although the studios have mainly been used for dubbing feature films and television programmes, major artists such as The Beatles, The Rolling Stones, The Who, The Jimi Hendrix Experience, Pink Floyd, Electric Light Orchestra and Deep Purple have recorded songs in that studio, particularly at their former premises at Engineers Way, Wembley, where Queen recorded demos in 1971.

We were putting some new material down that was a bit more jazz inclined, and Roy was experimenting with different time signatures and odd instruments etc.

One afternoon that stands out more than the rest was when we were booked in, I think it was studio one, at two o'clock.

As we walked in to the studio we realised that there were other people still in there using it.

We thought we had made a mistake with the time, and we started to walk out again, but someone told us to come on back in.

It was none other than Fred Astaire. He was just finishing off some overdubs, for an album he had recorded with Bing Crosby.

Bing had gone back to the States a few weeks earlier and Fred stayed on to put his tapping on.

It was absolutely magic to meet a legend like that.

He was so down to earth. He apologised to us for running over the time but we didn't care.

At his invitation we sat down and listened while he and the engineer finished off the track.

What a man! He even walked as if he was on the dance floor – he was so light on his feet.

We used that studio quite frequently, so we met a few artistes there. I remember Rick Wakeman was recording something there. We used to play pool at the little bar there. Also David Carradine was doing something there.

As the studio was literally next door to Wembley Stadium, Evel Knievel's driver and roadie used to come in for a drink.

I remember seeing his two trailers, parked outside. One was a huge luxury mobile home, with the stars and stripes in the upholstery, and the other was for his bikes, and I think he also had a car in there.

Unfortunately we never got to see the actual stunts with the buses, etc. We were actually gigging in between recording days, which were staggered.

Martin Kinch is an avid fan of the bands that Roy Wood was involved with over the years. He's a really nice guy and a collector of memorabilia of all these bands. He is also a radio DJ at Stoke Mandeville Hospital. He has an amazing collection of photos, singles, posters and interviews on his site, which is named after a Roy Wood song, 'Cherry Blossom Clinic.' You'll find loads of pics and info on Wizzard, Move, ELO and much more on his site. Check it out.

## FULL MOON

Keith Smart and I were invited to a music store in Tottenham Court Road to have some photos taken sitting behind two drum kits.

The whole thing was a promotional endeavour to entice us to change the brand of drum kits. So we went into the store and did our bit, posing for photos.

When we were through with that, we went upstairs to a small meeting room, and there was the man himself ... Keith Moon.

We chatted for a while, and took advantage of the small buffet and drinks (as you do), and carried on chatting. KM told us that after this thing, he was off to Shepperton Studios to rehearse with the boys.

He invited Keith and myself to Shepperton if we fancied it as they were being filmed while they rehearsed.

It was a real pleasure meeting Keith. He came across as a gentleman with an upper class accent.

We were offered a lift to Shepperton by this guy who worked for Premier Drums and he said he would drop us off at our hotel afterwards. We gladly accepted.

We went off to Shepperton and eventually found the soundstage that they were using.

The first thing that struck me was the size of the place. The boys were all on stage waiting for Pete Townsend to turn up. When he spotted us Keith got off his kit and came to talk to us. He then introduced us to the rest of the guys, John and Roger.

KM proudly showed me his kit; it was very impressive. He had helped to design the fittings on the bass drum to hold the nest tom - toms.

He very proudly demonstrated just how robust the fittings were by standing on them and rocking to and fro.

I was well impressed.

He then proceeded to show me the 3 huge trunks full of spares. It was like a mobile music shop.

He had snare drums, tom- toms, loads of cymbals, hundreds pairs of sticks...and so on

Eventually Pete Townshend showed up, and shortly after they started rehearsals.

There was a bit of friction on stage, due to Pete arriving late. And it escalated somewhat. I won't go into details, but they have been together for a considerable number of years, so they're bound to have their differences.

I have never been in a band where there weren't any disagreements, and I've been in quite a few.

Eventually the rehearsal was postponed and we went back to our hotel.

The second time I met up with the Who was when I went to see them at Wolverhampton Town Hall.
To say they were loud would be a gross understatement!
They were loud but brilliant!
When they came off stage I went backstage to say 'Hi'.
I was with my wife Annie and we went upstairs to the Green Room and waited for the boys to come in.
There was a long table with a white cloth against one wall. It had the remains of a small buffet and there were also a few bottles of wine, beer, water etc.
Eventually Keith and Pete came in and sat next to us on the sofa. We chatted a while about the gig and stuff in general.

Then the most extraordinary thing started to take shape.
It started with this young reporter guy, who came and sat along side us. He had a Walkman (well it was a while ago) and proceeded to record our conversation.
Now remember he never asked permission or anything, he just started recording.
After a few minutes Keith and Pete got up and said, 'We'll be back in a minute,' and with that they left the room.
Annie and I just looked at each other. Neither of us could guess what was about to happen.
Then Keith and Pete came back in the room and one of them was holding a jug of water and without a word being said they got hold of the Walkman and pressed the play button and proceeded to pour water over it.
Well, the face of the reporter was a picture and he started to laugh it off out of embarrassment I suppose.
Then Keith and Pete went out of the room again, at which point the reporter went to the end of the table

with the buffet on it and crouched down at one end of it.

He was predicting that when the boys returned the next jug was for him.

Then in they came with jug in hand and as they approached the end of the table he lifted one end up a little.

That was almost a cue for what ensued.

As the table was tipped up all the bottles slid off and someone, I'm not sure who picked a bottle and threw it through a window. There were bits of porcelain flying through the air.

It was at that point that Annie and I started to take our leave.

Now what I forgot to mention, was that I had already arranged with Keith that we would take him and John Entwistle and also a couple of their road crew to the Lafeyette, a night club in Wolverhampton.

So I waited in the car park in my Triumph Herald and the boys were going to follow in their limo.

Roger and Pete went back to the hotel so I was waiting for Keith, John and a couple of road crew.

When we arrived at the Lafayette, I went in first while the boys were parking. I spoke to George Maddox, who was at the reception area and when I told him that I had Keith Moon and John Entwisttle and a couple of crew with me he turned white. 'Keep them under control,' he said.

I'm not sure what he wanted me to do exactly.

So in we went, straight to the bar naturally before I could ask Keith what he wanted he got his roadie to get the round in.

That's how it was most of the night. He'd obviously given a bunch of notes to his roadie before they came in.

At the other end of the room there was a band just about to start. They were called Light Fantastic.

I knew the singer who is now a stand-up comedian whose name is Ian Sludge Lees.

They were a pure rock band and a bit theatrical, as they did this coffin act, where half way through their set a couple of roadies would bring on a coffin then as they went through a particular song the lid started moving then a hand slowly appeared (you can guess the rest). Eventually the face appeared with blood trickling down from the mouth to the chin.

It was all very corny but in those days it was accepted. As the band started to play we ventured upstairs and to another bar.

Now this bar was right above the stage and there was a little balcony that you could look over and see the band. Well!!! Before I knew it, the roadies lifted Keith and carefully lowered him upside down and held him there until the band below could see him.

As quick as a flash, Ian the singer, on seeing Keith's face looming at him said, 'I see we have a full moon tonight!'

Eventually they brought him back up.

Then we went downstairs again and the band had got to the bit with the coffin and the lid was thrown back to reveal the guy inside. Of course Keith had to get in on the act and he tried to climb in. Well it was all in jest and the band took it well. Later the band joined us at the bar and again Keith got the whole round in again via his roadie.

## CHARITY GIG WITH JIM

One summer Roy Wood got a call from Carl Wayne who was doing a summer season with Jim Davidson in Margate at the time.

Carl told Roy that he, Jim and the cast of the show were doing a midnight show for a Leukaemia Research charity and asked him if he fancied doing a short set. Roy agreed and got in touch with me and a couple of others but not the complete band and off we went to Margate.

We had a very short run through of the four or five songs starting with California Man.

Now, those of you who remember the song, it starts with a guitar riff, which ends with a big chord, then the vocals come in, 'Going to a party, meet me on after school' ... well Jim had warned us that there would be fireworks on stage and to avoid a certain area of it. When we ran through the riff, the guy in charge of the fireworks suggested that when we came to the big chord he'd set one firework off.

We had to wait for the actual performance to see it working and work it did with great timing.

The night went very well and among the rest of the performers were Susan Maughn ( Bobby's Girl) and the comedy actor Bob Todd ( Benny Hill show). He was very funny.

Carl Wayne did a great set on his own then joined us for a couple of 'Move' numbers.

When the show finished a few of us went down to the beach and it was just getting light.

Jim's manager, Laurie Mansfield (he's the chap who is on all the Royal Variety shows who greets the Queen) was still in his black evening suit with not a hair out of place.

So there we were with Jim's Rolls Royce parked on the beach, doors wide open, the radio playing.

Someone found a stick so we drew a bar and some stools in the sand then out came a primer stove out of the boot and a tin of tomato soup. Don't ask why Jim carried a portable cooker in the boot of a Rolls Royce! It baffled me too.

Next time I see him I'll try to remember to ask him; as if that wasn't crazy enough again from the boot, came some skittles and balls.

We stayed there for a while longer then we decided we needed some food after all, one tin of soup between all of us didn't go far.

It was now creeping up to seven thirty and we spotted a cafe that was in the process of opening so we made a beeline for it.

The owner must have thought all his birthdays had come all at once.

We went in and ordered the full English breakfast, but with a difference because we also ordered two bottles of wine.

Then eventually we went to our respective hotels to sleep it off. That's rock n roll!!!

The show generated around four and a half thousand pounds for the charity.

## THE OLD HORN'S BAND

There was a period just before the actual demise of Wizzard, when a few of us got together, just so we could keep in touch with playing.

So we formed this band, consisting of guitar, drums, bass, keyboard, two saxes and a trumpet, trombone and congas/percussion.

We didn't rehearse much - it was quite informal and we just had a good time. We played some jazz standards, some Blues and a couple of ballads thrown in for good measure.

Altogether a nice mixture of good music.

The nucleus of the band was: Bob Brady, keyboard/vocals,Roger Hill, guitar, Mike Burney, sax/flute, Nick Pentelow sax/flute, Mick Evans, drums, Andy Peate, trumpet and myself on congas/percussion plus the occasional guest now and then.

The name for the band came from the pub where we used to gig every Thursday, the pub is on the Queslett Road in Great Barr, Birmingham.

We eventually built up quite a good following. They came regularly every Thursday night.

We had some great musical moments there.

One of my favourite pieces was 'What a Difference a Day Makes,' an instrumental featuring Nick.

It was a version done by Gato Barbieri a brilliant saxophonist from Argentina (he played the sound track to the film 'Last Tango in Paris'). He has a unique raunchy sound.

Nick did his own version, which was amazing and it always knocks me out whenever we play it.

Alas! We couldn't keep the band together due to the other members having other commitments like paying gigs.

Many years on we got together again, as The Old Horn's Band to do a one off charity gig in a pub near Stratford on Avon in a little village called Aston Cantlow obviously with a slight change in personnel. This time we had two keyboard players, so as well as Bob Brady keyboard/vocals we had Phil Bond who doubled on accordion, the drummer was a young guy called Dave Wilkes and on double bass Tyron Bishop. You can see/hear that band on YouTube.

## TEETH'N'SMILES

My introduction to the Theatre World

The beginning of 1976 was not a very good time for me.

My marriage had just broken up and with very little income due to the imminent splitting up of Wizzard (not that it was a great source of income contrary to what the majority of the general public thought, and still think probably), I was forced to sell the house.

It was during this time that I received a call from an old buddy of mine, Gary Afllalo.

Gary was the vocalist and front man for a Birmingham group called Breakthru.

He is a mean blues-harmonica player too.

After many years on the Birmingham circuit, they split up and Gary later moved down to London, and ended up in the controversial musical 'Hair.'

I remember going down to see the show at the Shaftesbury Theatre.

It was a raunchy, fast moving piece of theatre, and the music was great; all those songs that are now familiar (to anyone over 40 that is).

After a while I lost touch with him. You know how these things are, although I must admit, I am usually quite good at keeping in touch with people.

Then, out of the blue, I got a call from him.

He'd been busy doing some recording sessions and gigs after 'Hair' had closed.

He asked me what I was up to and I told him that Wizzard was in the process of folding up and we weren't doing much in the way of live gigs.

It was then that he told me to get in touch with a lady called Patsy Pollock.

She was the Casting Director at The Royal Court Theatre in Sloane Square.

She was re-casting for 'Teeth'n'Smiles,' a David Hare rock musical.

The play had already had a successful run at the Court. I'm not sure why they were re-casting exactly. I think some of the cast had prior engagements to honour. So, lucky for me, she was holding auditions for a drummer for the show because it was due to transfer to the West-End in a few weeks time.

If I may digress a little, it's quite uncanny how things work out. They were holding auditions for 'Hair' in Birmingham in the late 60's and they were held at the Hippodrome, which is in Hurst Street and right across the street was a music shop called 'Wasp'. It was a hangout for loads of musicians. I popped in there just before I went for the audition. I went out of curiosity really. If I had got it, I wasn't sure about getting my kit off. As it happened I didn't get it.

When the audition finished I went back home.

Unbeknown to me, my old mate Gary Aflalo nipped in to Wasp looking for me, and the guys told him that I was across the road at the Hair auditions. So Gary came looking for me, but I had already gone by then.

Someone asked Gary if he would like to audition and at first he was a bit reluctant but eventually he got up and sang a couple of numbers. They asked him to come back again in the afternoon and they offered him a part. So he was in the original show in London for a good few years. That came about because he went looking for me. Such is life!

Now back to '76' ...Thanks to Gary I was off to London.

Without wasting any time, I called Patsy and made an appointment.

I was invited to go down to London and meet her at the Royal Court.

As instructed I went to Sloane Square.

I was feeling a little nervous as I made my way there, because theatre was a totally new ground for me, and I wasn't sure what to expect.

Patsy made me feel at ease right away.

She began to tell me about the production. It was a rock musical. A story of a rock group playing their last gig at the Cambridge University May Ball and the inter-relations within the band, focusing on the relationship between Maggie (Helen Mirren) and the band's songwriter Arthur (Jack Shepherd).

The cast consisted of Helen Mirren, Gay Hamilton, Jack Shepherd, Anthony Sher, Dave King and Karl Howman as well as Hugh Frazer, Andrew Dickson, Mick Ford and Roland Macleod.

Much to my surprise, I felt quite relaxed while reading the part of Nash the drummer for her.
I had never done this kind of thing before. I mean not even amateur dramatics.
I read a few pages, and we chatted...I read a bit more...I was by now totally at ease and that was it really. She told me she would be in touch in due course and with that I returned back to Brum.

A few days later, Patsy rang me asking me to go down to London again, this time to meet the playwright David Hare, and the Musical Director, Nick Bicat. The venue was the Queen's Theatre in Shaftsbury Avenue.

There was just a drum-kit centre stage and nothing else. I was introduced to David and we just chatted for a while; he asked me about the sort of bands I had played with etc. and just chatted generally.
Then, I was introduced to Nick. He asked about my musical tastes and influences etc.
Then after our little chat he asked me to play the kit...I was looking round for the rest of the band, 'So, where are the rest of the musicians?' I asked, but it was to be just me.
I remember thinking it a bit strange as usually when you audition on drums you play with the band, even if you just have a bit of a jam to feel each other out. But I thought, this is theatre I guess they do things differently, so I jumped on the kit.

Nick asked me to play a couple of different 'feels', (beats) and then he asked me to do a little solo.
I felt quite comfortable with both requests, and after a short solo I came down into the front stalls and we all chatted a bit more, we said our goodbyes and that was that. I left to catch my train back home to Brum.
I had no idea how it went really and what they were thinking (they didn't give much away while I was there).
Although I was hoping to get the part, I had no reservations really, because of not having been in theatre before.
Within a couple of days of my visit to London I received an A4 size parcel in a brown envelope. It was the script for 'Teeth 'n' Smiles.'

With it was a note to welcome me 'on board'...so to speak.
There was to be a change from the original cast, due to other commitments of a couple of people.
Martin Shaw was to play the songwriter, formally played by Jack Shepherd and there was another character written in, a pop star that our Manager (Dave King) had discovered played by Heinz, (ex Bass-player with The Tornadoes).
Now at this time I knew nothing about the theatre-world, so the only people that I had heard of were Dave King, because before turning to straight-acting he was a comedian, and he used to have his own TV show and the other of course was Heinz.
But that didn't stop me from having nothing but admiration for everyone. I still couldn't work out what I was doing here, a non-actor amongst these pros, but I received plenty of encouragement and I got on marvellously well with everyone.

We rehearsed in Primrose Hill for 3/4weeks in all.

I was fascinated watching these guys bringing the text from the paper to life, as it were.

There was me worrying about the few lines I had to say, compared to their pages and pages it was nothing.

During the rehearsal period I stayed with various friends, one of whom was Mac Poole, a great drummer and an old buddy of mine from Brum.

He lived in Turnpike Lane, North London, so it was easy to commute to the rehearsal rooms.

The rehearsals eventually moved into the Wyndham's Theatre, right in the heart of the West End for the last week so we could block the show.

As I mentioned before, all this was a whole new ball game to me.

The first striking difference that I noticed from the 'group' scene if you like, was the discipline and professionalism within the cast.

Punctuality was one of the key issues. You had to be in the theatre for the half, which meant at least 35 minutes before curtain up that was a deadline, and of course, we used to be in our dressing rooms well before that.

The show opened in the summer of 1976.

It was that blazing hot summer, and the matinee's suffered a bit.

I was on a drum riser, which was on wheels and at one point I did a little solo as the riser was moved forward past the edge of the stage. It actually overhung by a couple of feet. I remember one matinee when in the front stalls about six or seven rows back was Robert Morley and he had his fingers to his ears bless him.

At another matinee Karl Howman brought another well-loved gentleman of the British cinema as his guest, but he made sure that he sat him towards the back and that actor was the wonderful Alastair Sim.

We all used to drink in The Round Table, in the alleyway next to the theatre including the cast of Equus at the then Albery Theatre, now renamed the Noël Coward theatre.

The cast of 'Funny Peculiar' at the Lyric Theatre just down the road also used the pub.

We all used to finish around the same time.

There was Richard Beckinsale, Julie Walters and Pete Postlethwaite with their little dog.

I used to play with the little fella up and down the alley just outside the pub. He was a jolly little mongrel/terrier... Nice times.

Unfortunately the show only ran for 7 weeks or so.

It was an amazing experience and we had some laughs. I met some lovely people, and no, they aren't all 'Luvvies', most of them are dedicated pros.


There was one particular Sunday when Karl Howman was doing a reading of a play.

It was to be done in front of an invited audience and it was literally that - a reading with all the actors on stage and just reading their parts.

Karl asked me if I wanted to go, so I said I would as I'd never been to one before and it could be interesting.

It was held at the Hampstead Theatre in Swiss Cottage.

Warren Mitchell was one of the main characters.

I can't remember much about the reading or the plot, however I do remember that Warren had invited all the cast and a few friends back to his house for a party afterwards. As I was Karl's guest I was invited too.

His house was in Golders Green. As we arrived at the house, I told Karl that I felt a bit, not nervous exactly, but a bit awkward because I was not directly involved with the reading.

'Nonsense,' he said. 'You were invited, so don't worry.'

I got on very well with Warren as we had the same taste of music. He liked jazz, and had a great collection of records of that genre.

He played clarinet, so it was not surprising that one of his heroes was Sidney Bechet.

We chatted for a while about music mainly. He showed me his record collection. It was all on vinyl of course and very impressive it was too.

As it was the middle of summer, most of the party was outside around the pool so it was relaxing and I soon got into it all. The drinks were a plenty, so was the food. It was great!

At some point during the proceedings Warren told Karl that if he wanted to get stuck in to the drinks, to go ahead, and not worry about driving home. He said that there was an empty 2 bedroom flat next door to the house which belonged to his son, but he was away and we could both kip down for the night.

This suited me as I lived miles away on the other side of London and I did not have wheels.

So we both thanked him and thought what a kind gesture.

It was luxury - a bedroom each with all the facilities, and we could have a few drinks without the worry of getting stopped.

In the morning Karl suggested that we should not disturb them at the house so we were going to drop the keys to the flat through the letterbox as quietly as we could.

We had not gone more than a few steps from the flat, when there was tapping on the front window of the house.

It was Warren (I half expected him to break into Alf Garnett behind that window.)

'Where are you going?' he said. So Karl told him that we didn't want to disturb them. 'No' he said. 'Come in for some breakfast.'

So we went in and had breakfast and stayed and chatted, mainly about the party. We told them that the food at the party was delicious and that we had met some lovely people there then after a short while we said our goodbyes, thanked them again and we went on our way.

When 'Teeth 'n' Smiles' was over, I went back up to Birmingham for a short while, mainly to sort out the house and other bits and pieces.

I finally sold the house and just about broke even, what with agents fees and the fact that we weren't in it that long for it to mature in value.

Shortly after, I went back down to London.

## JAZZ IN BIRMINGHAM

As I stated earlier, John Killigrew's influence led me to listen to, and appreciate jazz and singers like Sinatra and Bennett etc.

So whenever there was a jazz concert on in Birmingham, I was there. I have seen most of the giants of jazz, people like Erroll Garner, Duke Ellington, Earl Hines, and Dave Brubeck - all with their own distinctive styles of jazz piano.

Buddy Rich, Louie Bellson, and Joe Morello - all amazing drummers. If I had to pick a favourite I'd have to say Buddy Rich as he had it all – technique, style and he made it look so easy. He has been a star since the age of four.

The best venue I saw him at was Ronnie Scott's because it's small and intimate but it must have been a bit cramped to get all his band on that small stage.

Ronnie's was definitely one of the best places for jazz. I've seen greats there like, Milt Jackson, Zoot Simms, Dexter Gordon, Bill Evans and many more.

I miss Ronnie's introductions, but most of all I miss his jokes. Before he actually introduced the main artist he would spend fifteen to twenty minutes cracking these old jokes and he delivered them with a straight, deadpan expression.

Here's one of his gags: he said this to a guy near the front of the stage, who was wearing a leather jacket, "That's a nice jacket sir, does that mean that there's a Ford Fiesta going around London with no seat covers?".

You had to be there to get the feel of his gags and the place itself.

## HONG KONG

I worked with Nick Bicat again, on a couple of occasions after 'Teeth' n' Smiles'. Some of the sessions that come to mind are, Howard Brenton's 'Epsom Downs' for Radio3, Paul Jones and Maggie Bell were also on the session.

Nick and I recorded some incidental music used for The National Theatre's production of David Hare's 'Plenty.'

A little later Nick was involved with a production for the Oxford Playhouse Theatre.

It was to be a rock-musical adaptation of Shakespeare's 'All's Well That Ends Well.'

Nick and his brother Tony composed all the music and lyrics for this show.

I was delighted to know that my old buddy, Andrew Dickson, would be playing guitar on this show.

The Musical Director was Terry Davies (piano) and the band consisted of two saxophones, a cello, bass guitar, guitar and of course, drums.

The plan was that we musicians would be used for a few weeks only to play in Oxford and Poole, then the Company, Nick and the Musical Director would go to Hong Kong for a month to take part in their annual Arts Festival.

I suppose it was because Andrew and I were used to theatre productions that we put more hours in at rehearsals. I hope this doesn't sound too conceited, but it's the way it happened.

The rest of the musicians were very good readers. I personally don't read a note, so they worked to rule so to speak. When it came to 5pm they downed tools; they played by union rules. I didn't believe in all that, so when it came to the 'Tech' (it's a long day, it's when everything is put together, lighting, costumes, re-blocking, and anything technical) that's usually the day that anything can go wrong and it usually does.

Andrew and I stayed on to help the Music Director and cast. Eventually after 3 weeks of rehearsals we opened at the Oxford Playhouse Theatre. We then went on to the Towngate Theatre, Poole in Dorset and eventually finished off back in Oxford again.

We gave a little sample of the show outside the Inn on the River pub on a hot sunny afternoon.

It was just after that little gig that Nick Kent, the Stage Manager asked Andrew and I if our passports were up to date.

He went on to explain that the cast would like us to go with them to Hong-Kong but the pay would be minimal, and obviously flight an accommodation would be sorted. Well! It took me just under a minute to think it over, and reply 'Love to,' and shortly after, Andrew agreed.

Richard Wilson was one of the first people to tell us that they were pleased that we decided to join them and he added that they would look after us at meal times. I suppose we could have said, 'We don't believe it,' but it wouldn't have got any laughs then. After all, this was the eighties and Victor Melldrew was not around yet. Richard played the King, Gaye Brown the Countess. Also in the cast were Phillip Joseph and Belinda Lang.

The cast flew out the following week and Andrew and I were to join them a couple of days later.

We flew by Thai Airways and the flight was around 15 hours and we made three stops: Frankfurt, New Delhi, and finally Bangkok, where we changed planes for the final leg of the journey.

Landing at Kai-Tak Airport is reputed to be one of the most hazardous tasks for pilots...On one side, quite close to the runway, there are blocks of flats, and a great hill, where Hong Kong is built. The actual runway itself is built on the water so it's a bit hairy as you descend onto the runway.

Well... that's the Geography lesson over with.


We were met by Nick Kent and were taken to the Holiday Inn, in Nathan Road, Kowloon. We were to stay there for a couple of days courtesy of the Hong-Kong Arts Centre.

Next morning was our first rehearsal. We were introduced to the two musicians, Gerald the Saxophonist, a Filipino, from Manila and Monk-Tom, as he was affectionately known, on bass who was, believe it or not, 70 years old.

The first day's rehearsal went quite smoothly. We got on well with both guys. You get a certain vibe as you start playing with a musician for the first time and this felt good.

At the end of the rehearsal, Tom disappeared for about 5 minutes and as we were asking Gerald if he could recommend somewhere cheap to eat, Tom returned and announced, 'Now we eat, yes?' Before we could reply he added, 'I have taken care, now we go.'

So Terry, Andrew, and I went with them and they drove us across to Kowloon through the tunnel.

The restaurant was on two floors. As we entered all the staff seemed to know Monk-Tom (there was much nodding and bowing going on) and we were shown upstairs to a big round table. There were two women and a couple of kids sitting there. Tom introduced us - they were their wives and Gerald's kids.

We didn't need to look at the Menu. Tom had taken
'care of it' and within minutes the food started arriving
... and kept on coming. There were dishes we never
knew existed, a bit different from your local High
Street Chinese back in the U.K, I tell you...everything
tasted delicious, and we were hungry men.
When the bill arrived Tom just signed it and that was it.
He refused to let any of us contribute anything
...'Welcome to Hong Kong,' he said. What hospitality.
Altogether we were there for 4 weeks.
After the first few days at the Holiday Inn, the director
of the plays representing the Oxford Playhouse
Company gave a radio interview, mentioning that if
there were any ex-pats out there that could offer
accommodation to two clean-living musicians, to phone
in.
They received quite a few calls all of which were
genuine as we ended up staying with a British couple,
Mr. and Mrs. Tinker. They lived in an area of Hong
Kong known as Gardine's Lookout, which is located at
Mid-Levels.
If you remember the Geography lesson earlier: Hong
Kong is built on a massive hill and there are three
modes of transport to get you up or down. Taxi, bus
and a funicular railway that stops at three levels: First,
Mid and it Terminates at The Peak where there's an
open-air restaurant with a marvellous view of Hong
Kong and Kowloon below.
The Tinkers were really hospitable. Andrew and I had a
room each and we both had our own front-door key.
There was a communal swimming pool.
All in all we did all right I'd say.
The company performed three shows altogether.
There was the one I was working on, also The
Recruiting Officer and a two hander Hello Good-bye.
The latter was performed as matinees and I did have
quite a few evenings off.

On about the third night, just after the performance, I made straight for the bar as usual. Now I know this is going to sound a little contrived, but it's the way it happened, honest.

I was sipping my lager, taking in the wonderful vista of Hong Kong and Kowloon by night, when this guy came over to me and said, 'It's Charlie isn't it - Charlie Grima?'

I looked at him a bit puzzled. 'Roger,' he continued, 'I used to be with B.R.M.B radio, remember?'

Then after a while the face became a bit more familiar. B.R.M.B radio was a local radio station in Brum, and I had done a couple of interviews with him in the old days of Wizzard ...`So what are you doing here?' I said. 'Holiday?'

'No, I work for radio Hong Kong now,' he said, and proceeded to tell me all about it over a few more lagers. He told me that he had a show on Saturday mornings and invited me on to do an interview so I agreed.

So on the morning of that Saturday I made my way to Radio Hong Kong, with a blazing hangover.

Somehow I got through it, with the help of a few courtesy cups of coffee. We just chatted about the Oxford Playhouse Theatre Company, and the shows we brought over etc... and he played a few records including a couple of Wizzard hits.

It turned out to be a really pleasant interview once the coffee took hold.

About the second week of our stay, there was a notice pinned to the board at the Arts Centre, inviting us all to a complimentary boat-trip.

It was organised by a woman who was involved with the Arts Centre.

We were to meet down at the harbour on the Sunday morning around 9 am.

Now this was no dinghy, I can tell you.

It was one of those huge Junks, complete with those big red sails. We were going to sail to Lantau Island, one of the hundreds of little islands that are scattered around this part of the world.

We were all treated like VIP's. You only had to nod your head and there was a drink put in your hand.

Below deck, there were the living quarters, complete with a double bed. It must have cost quite a few Hong Kong dollars to hire I bet.

Nibbles and drinks were on tap.

Then about midday we anchored a little way out from the island, and transferred to a small launch type of boat to take us across to this restaurant on the beach. More delicious food ensued.

It was an amazing day; we all thoroughly enjoyed ourselves.


On Saturday nights, there was a 7- piece outfit playing upstairs in the bar, led by the trumpeter Lee Tracey. Would you believe it? The keyboard player was a Brummie Dave Packer (they're everywhere) and he knew most of the musicians that I mixed with back in Brum.

Before the night was over I found myself 'sitting in' with them. It was great. They were really generous. It was a total jam session. I just laid down a beat, and it came together. This happened every Saturday night while we were there.

I really enjoyed those jam sessions.


One night, Monk Tom told us that he was taking us to see his son, who was the Musical Director at the Excelsior Hotel's Cabaret Room.

When we got there, (again everybody knew Monk Tom) we were shown to a table, and within minutes Tom's son came over to say hello, but he couldn't stay because he had to go and conduct the band. But before he went away he called a waiter over and signed a piece of paper, and made his way back to the stage and that's when we realised that everything was taken care of.

We didn't want to take liberties, so we drank a little slower than usual. The Cabaret was quite a mixed bag of talent. There were a dance-troop, a girl vocalist, and a juggling act etc. The guys in the band were very competent musicians.

We couldn't help but feel a little guilty about not paying for anything but we tried to buy Tom a drink and he declined our offer politely and said, 'No problem.'

When I said earlier that these Brummies are everywhere it couldn't be truer as sure enough we met yet another one.

He'd been away from Brum for 18 years. He spoke pretty good Mandarin, (one of the many dialects spoken here) and his girlfriend was a local.

One night after the show he asked us if we'd eaten on a Sampan...(I thought it was a kitchen utensil) then he explained that it's a small boat, and you hire it by the hour and you eat on it.

Well you know the old saying ...'When in Hong Kong... do as the Brummies do,' so off we went.

There were a few of us, Belinda Lang, Phillip Joseph, Dave and his girlfriend,and yours truly.

We drove to a place called Repulse Bay (honest!) and as we arrived, these women approached the car, vying for our custom on their particular Sampan.

The Sampans are hired out by the hour and you have to haggle to get the best deal and that's where Dave and his girlfriend came in.

So we got on one, after we agreed the price.

It had a few laid out tables complete with checkered tablecloths and floor standing ice buckets.

The owner paddled us around slowly, and as you move around, these other little boats with provisions on board side-up to you and you order. The first one had all sorts of fish, crabs (live) etc.. on board ... again you haggle the price and then we finally chose one fairly sized crab and some huge prawns, then it moves just a little way away to cook your meal, and also to allow another one to pull up with more goodies... drinks, fruit, cigarettes, chocolates etc.

When the first boat returned all the effort was worth it. I don't know what they did to those prawns, but they were absolutely delicious - all garlicky and oriental. Altogether, a fine culinary experience

On the subject of food there was a great selection of restaurants to choose from.
We were taken to a Korean restaurant one evening where you cook your own food. We were shown to a table with a cooking apparatus in the centre; it was like a metal dome with tiny holes and a flame underneath. You order your meat or seafood, then the waiter comes and fills the little moat at the bottom of the cooking dome and pours some soy sauce. They also bring a few more sauces to dip in a couple of which were very hot. It was an experience but I found it a little frustrating having to wait for your food to cook in front of you.

There's a district called Aberdeen (yes it's true) and there are two huge floating restaurants, one is the Jumbo and the other is The Shatin. We ate in the first one.
The bay is also home to a large floating community, in their various shaped houseboats.
A bit different from the other Aberdeen - 'Eh Jimmy!!'
They were massive inside and at a rough guess they must seat at least two to three hundred people.
We were there for a month and we had a great time; we met some lovely people.
I wouldn't have missed this trip for the world. Most enjoyable!

# GERRY'S CLUB

My old buddy Karl Howman introduced me to a place
called Gerry's Club way back in 1976.
Well, I've been going there since that time. When I
lived in London I went there quite frequently.
It originally belonged to Gerald Campion, the actor
known for his role as Billy Bunter on TV.
He went to live in France well before I started going
there, so I never met him.
In 1976 Dee Hammond ran the club; she was a tough
woman, but underneath it all, beat a heart of gold.
The members there were involved in showbiz in one
form or another. There were actors, agents, producers
and directors.
The atmosphere was really cosy and you got to know
people very quickly there; it was a bit like 'Cheers.'

When I first started going there, the premises were on
Shaftesbury Avenue, and now it's in Dean Street,
where it's been for the last 25 years or so.
I still nip in from time to time.
In the earlier days they had a pool table, and I was
always on it.
Nowadays it is run by Mike and Alison Dillon who are
two lovely people. They used to be members from
when I first started going there.
Then they took over the lease of the premises.
You still get a trickle of old regulars coming in from
time to time. Some of the regulars are:Burt Kwouk,
(Kato in the Pink Panther films), Eddy McPherson,
(Mother of Suggs from Madness), Struan Rodger, a
fine actor and always busy, Barry Palin, managing
director of a production company, (they specialised in
the production of corporate videos, he gave me a little
acting job once). Kenny Clayton, affectionately known
as KC, a superb pianist and musical director for Petula

Clark, Matt Monro, Sacha Distell and Charles
Aznavour.

He is an Entertainer in his own right.

I had some great times there.

I was in there one evening and Kenny was playing. I
was itching to play along with him, then I had an idea
and I remember thinking to myself, this is either going
to work, or I'm going to embarrass myself, but I gave it
a go anyway.

There was an Evening Standard newspaper on one of
the seats and when I found out that it didn't belong to
anyone present, I picked it up and separated it in two
bundles and rolled both up and used them as sticks.

I joined in with Kenny by tapping on the bar and we
got swinging and every now and then Kenny would
give me a little break and we received a round of
applause. Nice, but it could have gone the other way.
So in this case spontaneity ruled the day.

Another one of the regulars was Don Hawkins, a fellow
Brummie drummer/actor turned filmmaker and
scriptwriter. He had a little drum kit which he left set
up in a corner of the club next to the piano, and he
kindly said that if ever I wanted to use it to help myself.
He left a couple of sticks behind the bar so you
wouldn't get any Tom, Dick or even Harry messing
about with it.

Michael Elphick  (Boon) was another one of the
regulars and we got on quite well. He once invited a
bunch of us to his house in Willesden for a party. I
can't quite remember what the occasion was; I think it
was his daughter's birthday.

He had this old piano in the front room, which of
course I had to have a tinkle on; it was a little out of
tune but playable.

He later had that same piano shifted to Portugal where
he had a little bar as well as his villa.

I mentioned Kenny Clayton earlier. There was one evening when I was walking along in Soho and I turned into this pedestrian only street, which had a wine bar/bistro in it. The bar had a large glass front and as I walked by I looked in and there was Kenny playing this baby grand.

Well! I just had to go in didn't I?

He greeted me and we had a little chat in between tunes.

The place wasn't very busy and after a short while I felt that urge that I get whenever I hear live music - the urge to join in.

So I went up to one of the staff and I told him that I was a friend of Kenny's and could he get me a small saucepan from the kitchen. Well, his face went into puzzle mode!

Now I don't profess to have the powers of mind-reading, but I would safely bet that the first word that came to his mind was 'nutter.'

So I thought I'd better explain that I was a percussionist and would like to join in with Kenny.

At that point his face eased a bit and he went into the kitchen and came out with a medium sized saucepan.

So I sat down near Kenny and started playing. It was great and I could tell that Kenny approved, otherwise I wouldn't have carried on.

But the icing on the cake came, when, unknown to me, among the few people that were sitting in a corner, was Petula Clark, (Kenny was her Musical Director). She had her back to me then she got up and came over and sang a couple of standard songs. I was delighted with the whole thing.

Nice evening. I had sore fingers the next few days but it was worth it. I mean saucepans aren't made to be played like bongos… now are they?

Another drinking pal was Ed Devereux an Australian actor who played the ranger in the TV series 'Skippy.'

He was also a singer and he'd sung with the Count Basie Band once. He has three sons and they're all in entertainment in one form or another. Two are singers/actors and the other records music libraries. When the mood was right, you'd have Ed, Burt, Kenny and another chap whose name escapes me, all singing in a Barber Shop Quartet style.

I hope this doesn't sound too conceited but I'm in my element when I'm in the company of showbiz people. Don't get me wrong there are a few who are up their own a://@es.

But the majority are nice people. They have their insecurities the same as anyone, maybe more so when you think about it. They have to deal with rejections and cancellations when they go for auditions etc.

Gerry's is still in Dean Street and I try and visit whenever I'm in the area. A couple of years ago I was invited to their Christmas lunch as Mike and Alison's guest.

It was nice to see those who are still with us.


I had a short residency in a wine bar in North London. I was playing piano and singing covers mainly rock n roll and a few boogies.

It was a Sunday lunchtime/afternoon gig and an old mate of mine Mike Felix used to come and see me. He was originally a drummer but later went on to piano, then an after dinner speaker and comedian.

Mike was the drummer with a band in the sixties called The McGill Five. They had a hit with 'Mockingbird Hill.'

Mike sometimes brought with him Ronnie Frazer.

Now, Ronnie was an actor who had been in loads of British films and was instantly recognisable. He was in many a war, military type film.

He was perhaps best known as Basil 'Badger' Allenby-Johnson in the 1970s television series The Misfit.

Also shortly before he passed away, he played the comical 'Lord of Love' who read romantic poetry and pronounced on all matters of the heart on the Chris Evans TV show TFI Friday.

However, he was also a long-established character actor with films such as The Wild Geese, Scandal and The Killing of Sister George to his credit.

He came with Mike on a few occasions and we got on fine. He joked about me needing an agent, so I jokingly said, 'You've got the job, if you want it.'

Chris and Ronnie both used to drink in the same pub on Haverstock Hill, Belsize Park.

Sadly, a few months later Ronnie passed away.

The night before the funeral, I was down in Gerry's Club. It was a bit quiet that night. I was sitting there supping a beer when in walked Peter O' Toole. He was going to be one of the pallbearers for the funeral tomorrow. We had a little chat and I bought him a beer and I brought him up to date as to who had also passed away, that he may have known from Gerry's.

I went to the funeral with Mike Dillon and a few others from Gerry's Club. We all met at the pub first then on to the cemetery.

There were quite a number of people there; people like Kenny Lynch, Mike Felix, Sean Connery, Stan Webb (singer with Chicken Shack) to name a few.

After the service we all returned to the pub. I had a brief chat with Stan Webb and reminded him of a drunken night in Germany, where he was staying at the same hotel as me in the Wizzard days. He vaguely remembered. Well!! It was a few years ago.

## THE MAN IN BLACK

I'm fully aware that the above title is credited to the great Johnny Cash.

But it can equally be associated with another well-loved character at Gerry's, a Canadian voice artiste, Bill Mitchell.

He was one of the busiest voice artistes in London. He had a real low gravelly voice.

He voiced TV commercials like the aftershave 'Denim for Men' and also a few movie trailers.

He was always dressed in black, from shoes upward, plus a black hat, and tinted glasses. I bumped into him once in the street, and I happened to be wearing a black shirt and black trousers, but white trainers. So as I said 'Hi to him, he came back with …"Hey, you and I could do a double act". It's a pity that you f!!d up on the shoes"

I remember one time when I was involved in a puppet theatre production that was being filmed.

I was originally hired to play congas, because it was an African children's story, but I ended up composing and playing the main music theme, on keyboard/synthesiser as well as incidental links between scenes.

They were auditioning actors for the voices of the characters. One actor that got the part of this horrible looking vulture was Chris Fairbank, better known as 'Moxy' in 'Auf Wiedersehen Pet', and a villain in the first Batman movie.

Then they wanted a voice for the Lion, well we all thought of the same person - Bill Mitchell.

Dudley Sutton who was directing this thing, said that Bill would be ideal, but probably too busy, to bother with this low budget production.

So I said I know exactly where to find Bill and I'd have a chat to him.

As we were already in Soho in this little studio, I didn't have to go far to the Coach & Horses, another regular watering hole for actors and media people.

Just a couple of little facts about The Coach and Horses.

The landlord there is Norman, who is the spitting image of Walter Matthau.

The other fact is that the pub was the setting for a play called ...'Jeffry Bernard is Unwell'. It's a play by Keith Waterhouse about a real-life journalist Jeffry Bernard. Who used to write a column in 'The Spectator.' Jeffry was still alive at the time the play was first performed in the West End in 1989. Both Keith and Jeffry were frequent visitors to Gerry's Club.

The play was centered on Jeffry being accidentally locked in the pub, overnight.

Peter O'Toole made the part of Jeffry famous; he was absolutely brilliant when I saw it.

At some point later, Tom Conti played the part as well.


Sure enough there was Bill at the bar, talking to Nigel Davenport, a British actor, with a very memorable face usually plays military officers.

I waited till they finished talking, and then as Nigel left I went over to Bill, he greeted me with that gruff voice.

I came to the point and said 'I have a gig for you, Bill,' and then I ordered a couple of drinks for us.

'You have a gig for me - do I get to sing?' He said.

I don't know what made say "maybe" it just came out. Then once I'd got his interest, I explained the scenario and managed to convince him that, if anyone could bring this Lion to life, he could. I think it's called applied psychology.

I told him that the studio was just around the corner, and he could put down his voice in a few minutes.

To my astonishment he agreed.

So off we went and on the way, he stopped outside an off license and said 'Shouldn't we get a few libations to keep the throat moist?' I thought, that's one way of putting it.

When we arrived at the studio, everyone was agog; they obviously didn't think that I would manage to get him.

Well he went straight in to the recording booth, with script in hand, he had a little rehearsal, and then he went for a take. He brought that lion to life. He was done within twenty or so minutes.

A true professional.

Bill was staying with another old buddy of mine, Zoot Money, a great pianist and vocalist, he has a very bluesy voice. In the Sixties he led his own R&B group 'Zoot Money's Big Roll Band' that's when R&B meant Rhythm and Blues, and not what it stands for today, Rhythm and Bass.

Zoot is still playing; he is involved with three bands at least.

He's in an outfit called The British Blues Quartet, with Maggie Bell, he has a band that plays at the Bull's Head, in Barnes West London, plus he sometimes gigs with Alan Price.

## CLIVE'S BIRTHDAY

During this time I was doing the odd gig on congas/percussion, with Bob (keyboard) & Nick (sax).

We were doing pubs, wine bars etc.

We had a short residency in a wine bar in South Kensington (name escapes me).

On one occasion we met Polly Dunn, daughter of Clive Dunn (Dad's Army).

She came in to the wine bar with Clive, as it was his birthday. She came and chatted with us out of earshot of her dad, and said that it was a surprise for her dad; she had invited a whole bunch of his mates who were coming in later.

She told us she would give us a signal later to sing Happy Birthday, with the arrival of the cake.

So we got on with the gig, the first two people to arrive were Anita Harris, and John Le Mesurier. Altogether there were about a dozen in the party. It was a good evening, and a good time had by all. As we were resident there we left our equipment there.

As we were getting ready to leave I went and chatted with Polly, and as we chatted, I overheard John Le Mesurier saying he needed a cab to go to Kensington Church Street to call on his son. So I said that we go that way home, and would be delighted to give him a lift.

It was a bit cheeky of me, seeing as we came in Nick's car.

But I told Nick, and he was happy to give John a lift. In those days Nick had a Citroen C V - neat little runner.

John was grateful for the lift, we chatted on the way there, he told us the he enjoyed the evening, and he said that his son that he was staying with, is also a musician, and songwriter.

He came across as a really genuine guy. We dropped him off in Church Street Kensington, and then off we went back to our hovel, in Notting Hill.

While we lived in this basement flat, we used to have the odd one or two people coming to visit when they were in London, and as we were three musicians sharing one flat we knew quite a few people between us.

On one occasion Ozzy came by with a couple of the guys in his new band. He had just split from Sabbath. Bob Brady was in his first band with Ozzy, and he knew me from the Nechells Green Community Center in Birmingham, where Sabbath used to rehearse when they were called 'Earth.'

He was in London because he was about to start rehearsals with the new guys, in some rehearsal rooms not far from us, so he popped in for the afternoon.

Then he came to the pub gig that Bob and I, were doing that evening. I have to mention here that this was before he looked anything like he does now, so he blended in more then, if you know what I mean.

Another one of our visitors was Geoff Turton, the lead vocalist with The Rockin Berries for those of you old enough to remember, they had a few hits, one of which was 'He's in Town.'

He was in London to see some people on business that morning, and after his meeting, he called around to our flat.

We all had a few libations, as you do, and I'm not sure where it came from but we started to re-write the lyrics to 'There's No Business, Like Show-Business.' And it went like this:

*"We've no business in show business; we've no business at all.*
*Everything about us is appalling; everything we do is just a botch.*
*We're just like a drunk who keeps on falling, while he tries pouring another scotch.*
*We know people, like show people, we know people like us.*
*Yesterday they told us, we weren't worth a light, then we opened and they were right.*
*Please don't come tomorrow, cos we closed last night.*
*So let's all sign on the dole.*
*Oh where's my giro?*
*Let's all sign on the dole*

It's amazing what a few lemonades can do isn't it?

## PORTUGAL

In the summer of '95 I had an offer from Danny McGuire to visit him and his family in Portugal.

Danny you may remember was the bass player in
'Ghost.'

They lived in Portimao on the Algarve.

I decided to take them up on their offer, as I needed a
bit of break, so I packed a bag and my bongos, and
managed to get a cheap flight.

Danny met me at Faro airport and of we went back to
Portimao.

It was lovely to see Danny & Marita and their two
lovely daughters Hanna & Zennor again, after quite a
few years.

They really made me feel very welcome, and as a
bonus, I played bongos with Danny at all his gigs, (and
he worked every night). At most of his gigs people
thought that we must have rehearsed a lot because we
worked well together. No such thing! It was fun - no
pressure whatsoever and we just got into it and that
came over to the audience. Sadly we lost Danny a few
years ago.

I'm still in touch with Marita and her lovely daughters.
They're all grown up now. Hanna lives in Japan with
her husband and baby and Zennor lives near Bewdley
in Worcestershire.

I'm in touch with her more than Hanna.

Zennor is a very busy girl as she has her own dancing
school and she's also a mother of a 2 year old, so she's
got her work cut out. Nice people.


Back to Portugal…

While I was there, I wanted to visit a couple of other
friends who also lived in the Algarve.

They were Graham & Ann who ran a pub in Almancil
called 'The Rovers Return'.

I eventually found it and I wanted to surprise them so I
just walked in to the bar and ordered a drink. Graham
served me and he did not recognise me at all (I guess it
might have something to do with the fact that I had a
bushy moustache the last time he saw me, and now I'm

clean shaven, wearing sunglasses and to round it all off a straw hat).

So as he handed me the beer and I casually said 'Thank you Graham,' and he did one of those double takes.

It took a few seconds,…then the penny dropped and we chatted about my visit to Portugal and so on and then he called Ann who was upstairs and told her that there was a strange looking character in the bar. She was equally surprised.

It was nice to see them both.

Bob Brady and I used to play at the pub that they ran when they were back in London and each time they moved we kept Saturday nights free for them.

We had some of our best times in these pubs. The best one by far was Steptoes in Stoke Newington High Street; the atmosphere there was electric. We played it every Saturday and got to know all the regulars. There was a rowing team from Stamford Hill and the Smiths, 'a Liverpudlian family. The same people would come every week, and gradually they would bring new people with them.The place was packed every week.

It was altogether a really enjoyable gig.

A few days later that week I went to surprise another old chum, Michael Elphick, (He played 'Boon' on TV and also in 'The Elephant Man' and Quadrophenia) a drinking partner from Gerry's Club back in London.

I knew he had a bar in a little village not far from Faro, I can't remember the name of the village.

It was a quiet little place with a beautiful church in the centre of a square.

It was mid-afternoon and as I walked in I noticed two things; one was that it was mainly an English crowd in there and the other was the upright piano in the corner.

I immediately recognised it as the same piano that Mike had in Willesden as I had played it at a party that Mike had a couple of years before.

So I ordered a drink and asked for Mike. The guy behind the bar told me that Mike didn't own the bar anymore but he nips in from time to time.

I later found out that the guy behind the bar thought that I was a reporter and that was why he was a bit cagey when I asked about Mike. Anyway, I then asked if it was okay to have a little 'plonk' on the piano and he said it was fine go ahead. So I started playing a 12 bar blues, and was greeted with a round of applause. Well of course I then followed on with a couple more ' boogies' and someone then filled my glass again as I went into 'Blueberry Hill.' Of course as soon as you play the intro to that, everyone recognises it immediately. I had just finished it when I heard this deep voice from behind me saying.

'What the...what a pleasant surprise.' It was Mike.

He was pleased to see me, so I played a bit more, drank a bit more and had quite a pleasant afternoon.

He offered to put me up for the night so I wouldn't have to worry how late I stayed and all the regulars in the bar wanted me to play more, but I couldn't stay because I was expected back at Danny's for supper.

So I arranged to go back in a couple of day's time.


I did go back to the village one late afternoon.

I spent the evening at that bar again, and I took Mike up on his offer to stay in the spare room.

When it was chucking out time, both Mike and myself were a bit worse for wear, not only that but were pissed as well!

It was pitch black everywhere, not one single street light anywhere.

I just followed Mike. He'd obviously done this a few times, then suddenly he said, 'We turn left at this tree,' and then we walked along a shallow wall.

Now, Mike's villa was next door to Clive Dunn's; in fact we actually had to go through Clive's front garden to get to Mike's.

As we walked through Clive's garden, we saw him through his window. He was watching TV.

Mike tapped on the window, which startled him.

He quickly turned off the lights in the room. He was definitely startled. Then Mike said, 'Hello Clive. It's me, Mike. I'm with a friend of your Polly (his daughter). Sorry to startle you.'

Then he put the light back on and opened the door and invited us in, but Mike politely declined the offer. He'd had quite a few drinks and said he was tired. So we went in to Mike's villa.

I slept in the spare room and I got up quite early, so as it was getting light I wandered out to the pool outside. It was warmer than I thought it would be, considering the sun was just rising. I must have dozed off out there, because I remember being woken up by the heat of the sun and the strong smell of coffee. Mike offered me a coffee and we drank it out there. I was still hung over, relying on the coffee to sort me out. Shortly after I thanked Mike and walked into the village to get a taxi to the railway station to get back to Portimao.

## THE BUSH THEATRE

Early in '77, I met Mike Bradwell, founder of the Hull Truck Theatre Company.

He had seen me in Teeth 'n' Smiles, and got in touch with me because he was going to direct a new comedy by Bill Tidy and Alan Plater called 'The Fosdyke Saga.'

Bill Tidy based it on his strip cartoon in the Daily Mirror.

We got on really well. He is a typical northern chap and very passionate about theatre.

I was to play drums, and play a couple of parts in what was a hilarious adaptation of the strip cartoon.

The first cast was: Micky O'Donoghue, Philip Jackson, Penny Nice, Kevin Elliot and Malcolm Ranson.

We all went up to Leicester and the BBC came up to film it (I can't remember why Leicester, exactly). The director was Mike Newell, who is now a world wide known director of 'Four Weddings and a Funeral,' Donny Brasco,' Harry Potter and The Goblet of Fire' and 'The Prince of Persia'...just to name a few.

Mike Bradwell was also in Leicester with us, because he was going to direct the stage sequel, which was 'The Fosdyke Saga Two.'

We opened at the Bush Theatre London with a slight cast change. The part of Ditchley, which was originally played by Phillip Jackson (Inspector Japp in 'Poirot'), was now to be played by Jim Broadbent. (a very busy actor nowadays, on both sides of the Atlantic).

We then toured up north for a couple of months, which included Birmingham, at Gosta Green.

I remember my dear mother coming to that performance. Her English wasn't very good bless her, but the show was very funny visually, especially the Tripe Fight towards the end.

She seemed to enjoy it in spite of the language barrier.

I played drums for all the songs and also played a couple of parts, one of which was Sidney Greenfeet (a play on the name Sidney Greenstreet from the film 'The Maltese Falcon.')

As many of you may remember he was quite a rotund kind of person, so they got me to wear this inflatable 'belly' around my middle, which got the laughs as predicted. At a point in the play, Malcolm Ranson's character had to do a couple of karate moves on me. I felt completely safe because Malcolm was, and still is, a fight arranger, for theatre and film. The idea was that I as Sidney gets attacked by Malcolm's character, a couple of kicks, followed by a couple of punches to the stomach, of course very skilfully executed. But this one time, just prior to the 'fight,' I felt the belly deflating and suddenly I began to wonder if he was he going to notice in time.

Well, as the true professional that he is, he did, and he held back his punches and kicks, just short of touching...Perfect.

As the show was about tripe, we used to have real tripe for the fight scene. The tripe was cut up into hand-sized chunks and it was thrown all over the place. Sometimes little pieces were thrown accidentally on purpose at the audience.

It was all part of the fun of the show.

One venue that that sticks out more than the others was Rotherham. We arrived at the venue and set up as usual. We had a little rehearsal to get a feel of the stage area. We went through the routine as usual and just ran through the bit in the script where there was a gag between Malcolm and myself. It went something like this...

I'm sitting behind the drum kit, having just finished the song when Malcolm comes over to me and says, 'Can you send a message on those things?' and I reply, 'I'll try.' At which point I go into a drum solo for about 6 minutes and at the very end of it Malcolm asks, 'Well?'... and I reply 'There's nobody in,' which always got a laugh and applause.

So we were going through this routine and when we had finished I noticed there was a guy sitting at the back of the stalls. He must be staff we thought. He then came down and introduced himself. 'Hi, I'm Will Gaines, I'm a hoofer (showbiz term for dancer). Do you mind if I bring my shoes tonight?' he said in a broad American accent.

We didn't quite know what to make of him, so we were polite and said, 'OK, no problem.'

So in the evening the show was going well, lots of laughs in all the right places, then it came to the gag with the drum solo, Malcolm said his Line 'Can you send a message on those things?' 'I'll try,' I replied, and started my solo. Then, from the corner of my eye I see this guy we met this afternoon, making his way down to the stage and when he reached centre-stage he started tapping, so at that point, I played a little quieter (still doing the solo) and eventually I was playing on the rims of the drums. Meanwhile this guy was tapping up a storm and after a while I came off the drum kit still tapping with my sticks, on the floor this time, and I walked and played towards him, until I was by his feet, and we did this 'conversation with each other for a bit, at which point I started walking back towards the drums (still tapping) until I reached the kit. I carried on and meanwhile he starts making his way back to his seat to tumultuous applause, at which point I finished my solo, and Malcolm said his line "Well?" and I replied, 'There was nobody in,' and then another great round of applause.

Moments like that you could not rehearse.

I've seen Will Gaines a few time since then. I jammed with him a couple of times. One time I went up to the Edinburgh Festival, just as a punter, and saw that he was appearing there so I got a ticket and went in. I was in the third row which was an intimate little venue. He had a trio backing him, and after a while he noticed me, and he said to the audience "I notice that there's a friend of mine in the audience. Come on up here Charlie" So I did, but as I got up on the stage I had no idea what I was going to do, so I decided to sing a twelve-bar blues thing, and he tapped to it. Then I got a couple of coins from my pocket and started tapping with him. I just loved the spontaneity of it. When I had finished I just went back to my seat and watched the rest of his show.

A really enjoyable little interlude.

Will Gaines, last in a long line of Jazz Hoofers was born in Baltimore in 1928. He grew up in Detroit where he learned his craft with such greats as Lucky Thompson, Kenny Burrel, Tommy Flanagan and Sonny Stitt at the Apollo, New York, 1954.
The man is still knocking them out with his magic feet at the age of 81.

## THE FOSDYKE REUNION

I had lost touch with Mike Bradwell founder of the Hull Truck Theatre Co.
So I phoned Rachel Bell an actress friend of mine who knew Mike Bradwell.
Rachel is the wife of the late Mike O'Neil - a great musician, singer, and songwriter. I remember I was visiting Mike and Rachel one time coming up to Christmas and while I was there the phone rang. Mike went and answered it. He chatted for a bit while I talked with Rachel. Then after a bit Mike said, 'Charlie, come and say hello to Clive,' and as I got close to the phone, I put my hand over it and I whispered in Mike's ear, 'Who the heck is Clive?'
'Georgie Fame,' Mike said. So I had a short chat with 'Clive', then we exchanged season's greetings and I passed the phone back to Mike.

O'Neil was very talented musician. One of his specialties was to take a well- known saxophone solo and put lyrics to it - no easy feat.
He was from a place called Leigh in Yorkshire, as was his buddy Clive.
They were both similar in style as they were both into jazz and their idols were Jon Hendricks and Mose Alison.

In fact I went to see Jon Hendricks at the Opposite
Lock Club he sang 'Yeh! Yeh!'
Hendricks composed the lyrics and it became a 1965 hit
for British R&B-jazz singer Georgie Fame, who
continues to record and perform Lambert, Hendricks &
Ross compositions to this day.
So... to get back to the other Mike.
Rachel gave me Bradwell's number and I gave him a
ring.

The last time I saw Mike was when the Bush Theatre
was celebrating their 25th anniversary and they put on a
show, a bit like a review of snippets of some of the
productions they had put on over the years. Mike rang
me to tell me that they wanted to do one song from the
show that I was in for four months, 'The Fosdyke Saga'
and would I be available.
'Yup,' was the answer. I quite looked forward to seeing
the cast, as it had been twenty odd years since we did it.
We had a quick rehearsal on the day before.
We all greeted each other like a family reunion.
There was only a couple of the original cast that
couldn't make it. Those who did come were: Roger
Sloman, Malcolm Ranson, Penny Nice and
Jim Broadbent.
Jim started the song off then the rest of us came in.
There were loads of performers over the twenty-five
years as you can imagine.

It was fun to do, even though it was short and sweet.
Quite recently I decided to give Mike Bradwell a ring
just to catch up. He was pleased to hear from me and
after a bit of catching up on each other's news, he
asked me if I was free the coming Tuesday. I asked
why and he said that Helen his lady, who is a
playwright had written a play and it was being read on
Tuesday at a venue in Islington called The Union
Chapel and he invited me. He said that I would see my

old buddies Jim Broadbent, Phillip Jackson and Roger Sloman who were helping out with this reading.

The reading was in the afternoon. I saw Mike before the start of the reading and it was quite an informal event with all the audience consisting of invited guests. When the play was being read I have to admit that I missed a lot of it, due to the acoustics, after all it was a chapel with a high ceiling so it echoed a lot plus my hearing is impaired anyway.

But I did manage to get most of it.

It was very professionally done.

It was great to see Jim and Phil afterwards. I thought they may have forgotten me, but they both greeted me like a long lost brother. There were complimentary drinks afterwards and I chatted to Jim for a while, and that's when he told me that Sally, an old girlfriend of mine, had passed away. I'd forgotten that Jim knew the people that she lodged with.

After a while I said my goodbyes and thanked Mike and his wife Helen for the invite and went to catch my train back to Kent.

## COMMERCIAL BREAK

I knew Gary Holton (Cockney geezer in Auf Wiedersehen Pet) before he went in to acting. He used to front a band called 'Heavy Metal Kids.' We frequently bumped into each other when we were on the road.

I also worked with him in David Hare's production for TV called 'Dreams of Leaving.' It was just a walk-on part for me, but it was fun non- the less.

We had quite a laugh between takes; I think they were using real wine on the set, so we were a little merry at the end of the day's shoot. Then a group of us went back to his place and had a few more.

The next time I saw him was when he was appearing in a West End Musical called 'Pump Boys & Dinettes,' with Paul Jones and Kiki Dee.

After the show I went to a pub near the theatre, and had a drink with him. We sat down at a table where Patsy Pollock (Casting Director at the Royal Court) was sitting with a friend who was also a casting director. We just chatted about this and that and about the show. Then Patsy's friend looked at me and I sensed that she was hatching some idea and after a while she said to me, 'Would you be available for a casting tomorrow?' I was well surprised! I mean she'd never seen me before. I said, 'Yes, why not.' So she wrote down the details on a piece of paper, and that was that, and we carried on chatting again.

The next day I went along to the casting not knowing what to expect. Patsy's friend was there and she gave me a quick rundown on what it was all about.

It was for a commercial for 'Tonino Wines' and they wanted someone to pretend to play the trumpet.

Now, I'd never heard of the product.

It was a Sicilian wine and they would be filming in Sicily (of course where else?)

There were a couple of other actors waiting in the room and then someone came to get us, I say us, because they wanted to see us altogether: Howard, Anthony and myself at the same time.

We walked in and there were about six people in there. They showed us photos of where they would be filming and most of the photos had 'Mount Etna' in the background.

There weren't any instruments there, so we had to mime a trumpet, a saxophone, and a tuba.

They allocated the pretend instruments to each of us and told us to walk around the table, miming to a cassette player, playing this typical Sicilian street-band music.

The tuba was for Howard Lew Lewis (Elmo in Brushstrokes), the saxophone to Anthony Pedley and the trumpet for me.

The whole thing was a bit silly and we all felt a bit stupid doing it, but we soon got into it, then we sat down and chatted a bit, at which point I was very cheeky and asked for a cigarette, because I had left mine in the other room, and one of the guys offered me one, so I took it, thanked him, and that was that,...we said our goodbyes and left.

When we went out to the other room, Howard said to me, 'That was a clever little ruse there.' I had no idea what he was talking about. "Well, he continued, "they're going to remember you because of that thing with the cigarette".

I said, "I'm sorry to disappoint you but that was a genuine request, cheeky as it was but I had no ulterior motive other than that I was gasping for a fag".

I thought no more about it, then after a couple of days, I got a call from the casting director, telling me that I'd got it.

I was to fly to Rome on Monday, where we would pick up a couple of Italian actors, then on to Catania, where we would be based for the whole duration of the shoot. We stayed at a hotel which had amazing views of Mount Etna.

Our first day's shoot was in a lovely town called Taormina. It was a piece of cake! All I had to do was pretend to play the trumpet while walking around with the other two actors.

The weather was absolutely fabulous, especially as it was late November, early December and that's where I had my 40th birthday in that week (December 1st).

I went out to a nice little restaurant with a few of the cast. They very kindly got the waiter to bring a cake out with a few candles on it.

For me it was a bit like being back in Malta.

There were quite a few similarities to Malta including the people, the climate, the food,....after all, Malta is only about 70 odd miles away. In fact the Maltese come over to Catania to shop and return the same day and vice versa.

On the whole it was quite a pleasant little gig.

That was my very first commercial.

I later went on to do 3 other commercials:

One for TSB Bank with Arthur Smith, the comedian. We filmed in Chiswick outside and inside a real TSB bank.

Then we did a bit at Pinewood Studios.

I later did another one for 'Del Monte' Orange Juice, with Ray Winstone. We filmed this one at Pinewood Studios.

The set was a coffee bar set in Venice.

Ray was a Gondolier, with a cockney accent, (for comedic effect I guess) and he comes in for an orange juice, telling me that he'd had a rough day at work on the canals.

I pour him an inferior orange juice, at which point he refuses it, and says, 'No, I want a 'Del Monte,' then I pour him another, this time it's the real thing. I didn't have any dialogue, just eyebrow acting and polishing a glass or two.

It was a 40 second commercial and we filmed for nearly 10 hours.

The last one was for a chain of Steak Houses in Denmark.

We shot it in Camden, London.

Again I'm pretending to play trumpet (what is it with me and trumpets) dressed as a Mexican, complete with sombrero.

I forgot to mention that I had a moustache at the time so when I went for castings the other actors in the same room for the same job, all had a form of moustache of one kind or another.

That's showbiz!!

The Danish film crew chose this particular studio because it has a computerised camera on a big rig on the ceiling.

Also the studio was bigger than theirs in Denmark.

Still a gig is a gig as they say.

That completes my commercial work.


A lot later I had to shave my moustache off because they didn't want any moustaches on 'Mary Shelly's Frankenstein.'

More of that story later...

Because I was now clean- shaven, I had to have more photos done, so I had photos with and without moustache.

The answer of course is to buy one. There was a theatrical shop near the Post Office Tower that stocked wigs, moustaches and beards etc.

So I used to take it with me when I went for a casting for a commercial in case they wanted to see me with and without.

It looked quite real but I couldn't stand the smell of the glue at first but it got better.

## ENGLAND, ENGLAND

I was involved with another production for The Bush Theatre. This was a Musical about the Krays, called 'England, England', a Snoo Wilson play set to music by Kevin Coyne.

It starred Bob Hoskins and Brian Hall (the chef in Fawlty Towers) as the boys.

It ran for a short period at The Jeanetta Cochrane Theatre in High Holborn in August of 1977.

I remember that it was around the time that both Elvis and Groucho Marx died in the same week.

'England, England' wasn't a great show exactly, however it did give me the opportunity to work with Bob and Brian.

Bob played Ronnie; he was great to watch, both in rehearsals and the actual performances and Brian played Reggie.

The band was set up in the wings, out of sight from the audience. I was dressed from head to foot in a specially designed suit of feathers. I was a Falcon (yes I know, a Maltese Falcon) because when they were young they collected Falcon's eggs (I've no idea if it's true or not), so I had to appear every now and again, in their sleep. There was one amusing moment in rehearsals, which still gives me a giggle when I think of it.

Bob turned up a little on the late side, looking a bit flustered, anyway, we started the rehearsal, and a little way into the rehearsal we could hear this 'chirp chirp' sound. At first we all ignored it and carried on, then Bob stopped for a moment and apologised, and he proceeded to take this little sparrow out of his pocket. Apparently on his way to the theatre, as he went to get in his car, there was this sparrow on the pavement, with an injured wing, so he just picked it up and put it in his pocket and came to rehearsals. The poor creature was still chirping away, so at that point one of the theatre staff got a little box and took the bird and gently put it inside. 'Sorry about that.' he said. 'I couldn't just leave it on the pavement now could I?' So I thought I'd bring it with me.'

So with that sorted, we carried on with the rehearsal.


Within a few days into the show Bob was filming 'Pennies from Heaven' during the day and doing our show in the evening.

One night he was in such agony with his legs, his muscles had seized up after a hard day's filming, so we all said we would cancel the performance, but He said no, and a couple of the cast massaged his legs, and gave him a couple of pain relief tablets, but all the way through the show we could tell he was still in pain. One of the highlights of the play for me was when Bob had to fire a gun into a big crate-like box on stage. Well, at rehearsals and for the first few nights of the run, Bob used a stage gun, which fires caps but it wasn't dramatic enough.

So I suggested doing the shot on the drums.

The next day we rehearsed it just before the show, and it worked brilliantly

I watched him intensely at the moment he was to fire the gun, he looked straight at me as he was facing upstage (the audience were none the wiser) and using both sticks (the thick end first) I brought the sticks down from higher than normal, plus the two bass drums at the same time and it was so loud it made a couple of the people in the front stalls jump, but it worked so we kept it in. Needless to say that show didn't run for too long but I kept in touch with Bob and Brian.

Sometime a lot later Bob was in a production of 'The Duchess of Malfi,' with Helen Mirren and Pete Postlethwaite.

It was a lengthy piece with lots of blood and gore.

The venue was The Roundhouse, in Chalk Farm Camden.

I went to the opening night.

After the play finished I went to the bar and ordered a scotch for myself and a large vodka & tonic for Bob. When he came into the bar he didn't see me straight away because a few friends of his greeted him. So I waited till he was free and I went up behind him and tapped him on the shoulder with his drink in my hand. He turned round and I put the drink in his hand. 'Hello my son,' He said, 'Are you working here then?' 'No I said, 'I came to see the play.' To which he said, 'You didn't sit through three and a quarter hours of that, did you? Here, let's get you a drink my son.' And we both went up to the bar.

We chatted a while then he said that there was an after show party and told me to hang around.

So hang around I did.

I remember seeing Julie Walters and Pete Postlethwaite and the little dog was on Julie's lap. I went to stroke him but he'd obviously forgotten me and showed me his teeth, but he wasn't smiling.

I stayed for the party and I got well merry! I wasn't driving in those days so I sipped a few scotches.

The party was in the backstage area.

I remember playing some saucepans hanging up in the kitchen backstage. The rest of the night was a bit of a blur but I remember Bill Nighy singing along while I played on those pans.

I kept in touch with Bob; after the show closed, I went to see him in a couple of productions at the National Theatre.

I remember going to the opening night of 'Guys and Dolls' at the National. Bob played Nathan Detroit the rest of the cast was: Ian Charlston, Julia McKenzie and Julie Covington.

Bob gave me a pass to get me in to the party afterwards.

I consequently saw him in a few productions. He always got me a comp, which was very generous of him.

I also used to nip around to his house when he lived in Islington.

I went to see him around the time I was working with blind and visually impaired children / students. He was a big name by this time having done 'Roger Rabbit', 'Long Good Friday' and 'The Cotton Club,' so there was this major star nipping down to the corner shop to get some milk to make a cup of tea for us.

When he returned I said, 'Bob I need a little favour.'

"Sure my son what do you need, money?"

"No" I said, "Just a couple of signed photos for the blind kids that I'm working with, for their living quarters."

Then there was a pause...

"Here, are you winding me up?" He said in his gravelly cockney accent.

"What do you mean?" I said. "Well! If they're blind, why am I signing them?"

Good point I thought. "Well, because I will tell them that the photos are signed by you moreover some of the kids do have a little vision, plus we can write in braille underneath the photos."

I think that helped to clear things up, and we had a little giggle about it.

He told me he'd ask his secretary to sort some photos out and he would sign them.

True to his word two days later I received half a dozen signed photos, which the kids were delighted with.


I also kept in touch with Brian Hall. I actually worked with him in a variety show, which we took to France. It came about because Brian used to perform in a variety show once a month at The Theatre Royal in Stratford in East London.

He used to do a Max Miller impression, as well as a couple of music hall songs.

Well, I got a call from him on one occasion and he told me they needed a drummer to play with the pianist of the show.

We had a rehearsal, and that's where I met some of the performers: Kate Williams ('Love Thy Neighbour,' 'Poor Cow' Quadrophenia) and Christine Pilgrim singer/actress were two of them.

The pianist was Dave Brown and we got on great, right away. The idea was to take a holiday with pay. The venue was a caravan and chalet centre in the South of France, near St Tropez and Port Grimaud. It was run by a couple of English brothers.

I think they knew one of the cast. I can't quite remember the connection but it's actually not that important.

So after a couple of rehearsals in Stratford East, we went off to France.

Things didn't quite go to plan. First of all we found that there was not an actual theatre to do the show in, but we were all determined not to let it get us down. Brian had brought his family, and Kate had brought her daughter Kelly.

So we were going to treat it as a holiday and for the first couple of days we didn't perform at all.

Then someone suggested we do the show right there on the campsite bar area.

So we set up a little stage area (it reminded me of those old Mickey Rooney and Judy Garland movies, 'Why don't we do the show right here'). We did just that, and it went down quite well; there were many Brits on the site and they enjoyed it.

Of course Brian was recognised from Fawlty Towers all the time. Together we had a good time as it was like a little family.

## VARIETY NIGHT

As I mentioned earlier, Kate Williams was the Compere/Director for a Variety Night at the Theatre Royal in Stratford East, London. The show was on one Sunday each month.

I had been to see it a few times and I loved the whole concept of it. It was a very pleasant atmosphere in the theatre and the bar afterwards.

On one of these occasions I was in the bar after the show, I was talking to Kate and she asked me what I was doing gig wise. I told her that I was doing a few gigs on congas and occasionally drums. Then I mentioned that I'd also started doing the odd gig on piano and vocals. She seemed surprised because she only knew me as a drummer. So she asked if I would be interested in doing a little spot on the Variety Night Show.

Obviously I said I would love to.

True to her word she called me a week or so later to tell me that I was on the next show if I wanted.

I was a bit nervous at first because it was a theatre and a bit different from a pub in as much as the audience were all seated and more attentive than a pub. But I needn't have worried as they were a great audience and with me all the way.

Consequently, I went on to do more shows.

At one of these shows the top of the bill act was 'The Jive Aces'- a great bunch of guys.

When I finished doing a sound check for my spot one of the Jive Aces approached me and asked if I would be interested in going on a short tour of Germany with them as their pianist was going to Australia shortly.

I thought they were pissed or something!

I later discovered that they don't drink as they're all scientologists.

So what I'm trying to say is, I was both surprised and flattered at the same time.

I remember saying to them that I was willing to have a little rehearsal with them, and see how we got on. Had it been on drums I would have not given it another thought, but on piano I was still a bit shaky.

So they set up a rehearsal somewhere on the Holloway Road, North London and we cracked on with it. The rehearsal went better than I anticipated.

The next thing I knew, I was doing a gig with them in 'The Dove' in 'Broadway Market' London and we drove to Dover the same night to catch a ferry to Germany.

Our first gig was in Wuppertal. What a gig that was! The crowd wouldn't let us go back to our dressing room until we did an encore.

The small tour was great. I had my 48th birthday there in Mainz and the boys tried to give me the bumps in the middle of town with all these shoppers staring at us, but the boys gave up after the third or fourth one, thank goodness. I still go and see the boys from time to time and most of the time I get up with them on bongos. They're very entertaining to watch and they're constantly working.

Nice guys all of them.

## THE MALTESE PADDY

The exact date escapes me but let's just say sometime in the eighties I went to see a band playing at the Weavers Arms in Stoke Newington in North London.

Ron Kavana, guitarist, vocalist, songwriter and poet, fronted it.

The band's style is not easy to describe accurately, but I'll try.

The lineup was: drums, guitar, bass, fiddle, accordion, two élan pipes and Ron himself on guitar, bazooka and vocals.

So it was quite a sound. They played Irish reels and jigs, but with a rock feel.

I had seen them a couple of times, and they used to pack the place out.

I always carry my bongos in the boot of my car and one occasion when the band finished their first set I went and had a drink with Ron. We greeted each other then he said, "Have you got your bongos with you?"

"Yes they're in my car," I replied.

"Well get up with us on the next set then".

Well I don't need to be asked twice and I was up there when he called me up in the second set.

It went a lot better than I expected considering I was just busking it.

There were a couple of what I call 'magic- moments' when you're playing along and from nowhere, you and

another prominent instrument are 'talking to each other'
- that's the best way that I can describe it. After the gig
we had a drink together. I already knew Fran Byrne the
accordionist because he was a drummer as well and he
had been in a band called Ace.
They had a hit with "How Long has this been going
on."
Then Ron asked me if I fancied doing some more gigs
with them using congas as well as bongos and general
percussion.
That was it! I was in the band and that's when Ron
started calling me 'The Maltese Paddy,' or sometimes
Mick...I'd been called worse...so I took it as a
compliment.

We did a few gigs in and around London then we went
on a small tour of Scandinavia.
We played Oslo one Friday night, and because there
was some big football match on the following day,
most of the cheap hotels were fully booked so the only
decent hotel that the promoter could get us booked into
was this posh five star one (he was paying), so we
didn't mind.
In the morning we had to rush to catch the train to
Bergen, which is about an 8-hour journey.
We went on an absolutely wonderful scenic train
journey
I would recommend that train journey to anyone. The
scenery is breathtaking.

The only gig that was a bit iffy was in Copenhagen. It
was in an area called Christiana. The whole area is full
of drug heads; apparently it's not a secret. It's well
known to the authorities and the residents sell dope in
the street quite openly. They're all wandering round in a
daze. It was like watching 'Thriller'. I then realised that
they were going to be our audience.

I did not enjoy that particular gig at all. But in all fairness that was the only dodgy one really.

Norway was great. We played in Bergen and when we finished the gig Ron went out to the bar before me.

I was still in the dressing room when Ron came back in and said to me, 'There's a couple of your mates out there.'

'What do you mean?' I said. 'I don't know anyone in Bergen.'

'It's Slade,' He said, 'Look, those two guys at the other bar.'

So I went over to them and I said are you guys with 'Slade? Are you the road crew?' They looked a bit dejected. 'No I'm the guitarist and he's the singer.' one of them said. Then the other one said "You're Charlie aren't you?" I used to come and watch you play at The Railway in Curzon Street in Brum.'

Then they explained that they were the new line up of 'Slade.' Dave Hill, guitar and Don Powell drummer, were back at the hotel. I apologised for calling them roadies and we all had a giggle. Here's a coincidence. It turned out that we were all staying at the same hotel. I did not know until the morning at the breakfast table. Small world or what?


Sometime in the '80's Fats Domino was over here in the UK for a small tour. Alas I couldn't catch any of his gigs, due to my commitments at the time.

When the tour came to an end Fats and some of the band flew back home to the United States.

However Lee Allen, the Saxophone player and the bass player (sorry, name escapes me) were the only two that stayed on for a few more days in London.

They were both staying with a couple as their guests. This couple had organised a little private recording session at the 100 Club in Oxford Street for Lee Allen the bass player and some of Diz Watson's band.

Now, Diz is a great boogie piano player/vocalist. He had a band called 'Diz and the Doormen.'
The band used to play the London circuit they were a rhythm and blues outfit doing 'Professor Longhair,' Dr. John and some Fats Domino songs. So this couple got in touch with Diz and asked him if he and some of his band would be interested in backing Lee and record about 5 or 6 numbers.
Diz agreed and gave me a ring and asked me to play some percussion alongside Kieran O'Connor his drummer.
Well!! I jumped at the chance.
Lee was just writing tunes as he went along; they were mostly shuffles but very enjoyable stuff.
Lee is on Fats Domino's hits 'Blueberry Hill,' 'Ain't that a Shame' and loads more.
Allen also was the sax soloist on most of Little Richard's epochal hits from 1955 and 1956. On his own instrumental song 'Walkin with Mr. Lee.' I was only playing percussion but it was a satisfying session.

A few years later I was living in Finsbury Park in a place I detested. That had to be my lowest days ever. Ugh! One day I got a call from an agent that I had never heard of. He asked me if I was free to go to Norway for a month. At first, I thought that someone was taking the piss. So I asked him who he was as I had never heard of him. He then told me that he got my number from a mate of mine who was also a piano/vocals act.
I told this guy that he'd never heard me play, so how could he get me work? He said that this mate of mine had recommended me. So then I asked him when did he expect me to go? He replied, "Tomorrow, if I can get you a flight". He said he'd ring me later that afternoon. Sure enough he rang back and told me that he had booked me a flight.

This next bit was like something out of an old black and white spy film. My instructions were:

I was to go to Heathrow, go to the check-in desk, quote a number, get the ticket and when I arrived in Bergen I was to catch a number 03 bus to the market square, then I was to go into a place called Zachariasbryggen, which is a shopping mall and inside would be a piano bar with an English pianist/vocalist performing. I was told to wait near there where I would be met by an agent (theatrical that is) who would give me more details.

After a few minutes this English guy came up to me and introduced himself.

The place I was booked to play was a piano bar on a little island called Stord, which is about an hour away by catamaran ferry and the last one had gone ten minutes ago. So he waited until the pianist stopped for his break and he introduced us. That's was when he told him that I would be sleeping on his settee that night and I would catch the ferry in the morning. As you can imagine by now I was beginning to think that maybe this gig wasn't such a good idea. When the pianist went back on for his last set I got up and sang a couple of blues songs with him. When the guy finished his gig, I went with him to his digs and when we got there we had a couple of drinks and I told him how I got to be there. He turned out to be from Nuneaton and he was doing a month in this place before he went off to another gig at the next piano bar. He said he was missing home, and his girlfriend but he couldn't afford to turn work down. He showed me a list of the songs he had to do and that's when I knew that I was going to run into problems because most of the stuff that I play is more rock 'n' roll and blues. But I did mention that to the guy who sent me out there in the first place. Needless to say I didn't sleep easily that night. Next day I managed to get the ferry to Stord.

The place is a tiny island. The piano bar was in this place called 'Sjøhuset' - I think it means house by the sea. I walked in the place and was greeted by a guy calling himself Jon. He was the barman come bouncer. He showed me the piano bar, which was on the next floor up. There was also a restaurant on the same level. Then after a while he took me to see the sleeping quarters, which was a hut a little walk away from the gig. I dumped my stuff there then we went back to the gig and he said that I had to give him my passport, which he had to take to the police station in a couple of days. The first night wasn't too bad. There weren't that many people in and I just did a few laid back things really. The day after my fourth night, Jon called me into the office and told me that the police wanted me to go to the station because they want to talk to me. Gulp!! What now, I thought? When I got to the station they were very polite but it turned out that I couldn't work in the country with my passport, as I have a Maltese passport and at that time Malta was not in the EU. So I would need a visa to work there. So that was that! They said that they were aware of the agent doing this kind of thing before. They told me that I was very welcome to stay in the country as a visitor but not to work. Well it was very nice of them but where would I sleep? Because the bar would have to replace me as soon as possible and there was only one bed in the hut. It was a complete balls up. I quickly got on the phone to the guy who sent me out there and told him to either change my return date on the ticket or I was getting the first plane home and paying for it with his commission. He somehow managed to get it changed and I flew home the next day.
Never again!!!

# CRUCIBLE THEATRE

It was one winter in the 80's when I was involved in a children's play with songs - a little bit like a Panto really.

I was playing drums and percussion and the theatre was The Crucible in Sheffield.

The show started with me doing a brief drum solo, mainly to get the kids attention, and settle them down.

I can't quite remember the synopsis of the story, however, I do know that everybody lived happily ever after, as they do, and the kids thoroughly enjoyed it.

I recall the time that one kid wrote in to the theatre and asked if 'the drummer' was bionic. I didn't know if that was a compliment or not.

We performed the show in the afternoons only because in the evening the same stage was set up for the main play: Alan Ayckbourn's 'Bedroom Farce.'

As I mentioned before, it was a severe winter with 6 or 7 inches of snow. There was one performance that really sticks out; well not so much the performance, but more about what happened after the show.

The snow got worse. There were no buses, the trains had stopped and only people that could walk to their digs made it. Some of the others in the cast and myself had digs quite a way away from the Crucible Theatre. Some kind soul suggested that if we wanted to, we could stay in the theatre overnight.

They would have to lock us in of course. We all agreed that it was the only thing we could do under the circumstances.

The stage had already been set for the evening's performance, which of course was cancelled, so there were three double beds on stage.

We had quite a laugh during the evening.

We played some theatrical games, we talked about our backgrounds, and productions we'd been involved in, little anecdotes...and so on.

We passed time in this way for hours.

Eventually some of us were getting sleepy and grumpy and we knew that enough was enough, and we needed sleep.

We drew lots to determine who would be lucky enough to have a bed that was on stage, and the others had to make the best of wherever they could.

Guess who ended up in the stalls? Still it was a little exciting adventure I suppose.

Now when I watch the Snooker on TV live from The Crucible, Sheffield, it brings it all back to me.

One of the actors in this production was John Dale. If I remember right he also directed it.

It was only a short run, but I kept in touch with John, and a couple of months later, he rang me.

He was directing a few episodes of 'Playschool,' for the BBC, so he wanted some congas and general percussion on some of the episodes. I did about 6 episodes, …let's see now, I've looked through the Round Window...Square Window... Anyway it was fun to do. We used to rehearse in the BBC's own rehearsal rooms somewhere near Acton.

Then, when we went in to the studios we would record a couple of the shows on each day. It was fun.

## THE BILL

One time I was standing outside the French House, another drinking hole in Soho, having a drink when an old actor pal of mine Paddy Fletcher came walking past.

He was with his writing partner, another actor whose name was Richard Le Parmentier; he was an American actor.

Richard is best known for his role as Admiral Motti in Star Wars Episode IV: A New Hope, and the acerbic police Lt. Santino in 'Who Framed Roger Rabbit'.

As they came by Paddy said, 'We've been trying to get hold of you but no answer from your home phone.'
I was about to get a different mobile phone at that time so it was difficult to get hold of me when not at home.
Anyway, Paddy continued, 'We've just submitted a script for 'The Bill', and you're in it. Are you interested?'
'Sure,' was the only answer I could think of.
'It's not a huge part,' he said, 'You're a market stall holder selling dodgy perfume when all of a sudden this fight breaks out between some Skinheads and Mormons and you get knocked down to the ground while trying to protect your stall and stock.'
Not exactly, I was going to say 'ground-breaking stuff' but that would be too much of a pun, so I won't.
Anyway, I enjoyed filming it.
The whole sequence was well choreographed by Doug Robinson who's been in the business for years. He has worked as a stuntman and fight arranger on loads of movies, including 'Ben Hur,'so I knew we were in safe hands.
Most of the filming was done with a hand held camera especially this episode because of all the action.
I was finished by the early afternoon from an 8am start.
If that was a movie set it would have taken all day.

## THE OLD RED LION

I was in a fringe play at The Old Red Lion at the Angel Islington.
It was a showcase for new up and coming writers.
The play was called 'Clay.' It was a very funny piece about a husband whose wife thought he was having an affair with his secretary but she wasn't sure.
His wife was into clay modelling and she modelled this head, which came to life, but only the wife could see it, hear it and talk to it.

One evening the husband invited his secretary around to discuss some work which was quite urgent and as the three of them were drinking wine and chatting, the 'Head' was telling the wife how to get rid of him by poisoning him etc.

The 'Head' continues to slag me off goading the wife to think of ways to get rid of me.

I realise it may not sound that funny the way I'm describing it'; it has to be seen really. It was quite fun to do.

Julie Balloo, who at the time was Paul Merton's girlfriend, wrote the play.

He came to see it one matinee, as I remember.

Quite a few years later I was at Gerry's Club and Paul was also in there, at the other end of the bar. He kept looking at me as if he was trying to figure out where he'd seen me before.

So I went over to him and he said, 'Where do I know you from?' And I told him about 'Clay' and then he remembered and we just chatted over a couple of beers.

I did another play at the Old Red Lion. It was strange how I got involved really.

I went into the pub one lunchtime, and after I got my drink and sat down within a couple of minutes this guy and woman came up to me.

One of them asked me if I was working at the moment. I was taken aback and I told them, 'No, why?' They went on to explain that they are rehearsing a play at the moment and they are due to open in the next couple of days but they have lost their lead actor for reasons they didn't go into and would I help them out?

They said they had seen me in 'Clay.'

My immediate thought was, I'm never going to learn the script in two days and I told them so.

'It's ok you can go on with the book,' the woman said.

She was the director. I said I had never heard of such a thing. She assured me it would be ok, because they would make an announcement before the start of the play to say that I was helping out and would be going on with the book.

Well! … I thought I would give it a go.

It's not as easy as it sounds especially when it comes to handling props - very awkward I can tell you.

I'd put the script down on a table, pour out a drink say the next line…pick up the glass …you get the gist.

Still I gave it a bash and after the second day it was easing a little bit. It ran for a few more days. Phew!!! It was embarrassing at times even though they'd made the announcement before each performance.

## GROUCHO

I did two jobs as Groucho Marx. One was just a photo-shoot in Portsmouth.

It was for a CD cover of a band called 'Morphine.'

They had a track on it called 'Groucho' and they wanted me as 'Groucho' on the cover.

It was an easygoing gig really. I was dressed as a schoolteacher with the black gown and mortarboard hat and the usual Groucho make up. I still have the glasses.

The whole shoot took about three hours and I was back home in London, late afternoon.

The other one was a corporate video for Marks and Spencer.

It was done to make the clothes designers aware of the 50 year olds and to cater for them.

It was a two-day low budget shoot with eleven pages of script.

The script was very technical, mainly dealing with: percentages, pie charts and so on.

We filmed it in what used to be the Yugoslavian Embassy, which was down the road from the Albert Hall.

It was completely empty and it had a sweeping staircase on which they placed mannequins on every other stair.

The director was a young lady and as well as the written script, she wanted me to ad-lib a few 'Groucho' type quips. So I did just that: 'Do you follow me? …Well stop following me or I'll call the police!'

There was one scene where I came down the big staircase and stopped to talk to each mannequin in turn, and just as I got to the last one I f***ed up. So off we went again to the top and started again. Eventually I had to resort to the old cue card technique just for the last one.

It's not easy this acting lark.

They later interlaced the footage we shot with footage of interviews with Zandra Rhodes, Terence Conran and I can't remember who else. It was an experience to say the least.

I later did a small part in a graduation film for yet another female director who this time was a student at The Beaconsfield Film School. I played a tramp, who was sleeping rough in a barn and while I slept someone lit a fire encircling me. The rehearsal was ok, but when we actually went for the take proper, they literately lit this fire all the way round where I lay. It got a bit hairy I can tell you.

Still we managed to get it done and in the can as they say.

I wouldn't mind but the pay was almost non- existent. There was this actor who played a heavy Frank Scantori who I kept in touch with.

Sadly he passed away recently. I don't know how he died exactly.

Frank and I have a mutual friend, an actress Portia Boorof, who coincidently I first met years ago at an 'Acting for the Camera' course.

We've stayed in touch since and we meet up from time to time and catch up.

She's a very talented actress - she just needs a break, which I'm sure she'll get someday in the near future. She has a healthy CV and has quite a few productions under her belt.

## EXTRA EXTRA

In the 90's, I joined a union called FAA (Film Artists Association).

It's a union for extras in the film industry. I then registered with a couple of agencies. One was Central Casting and the other was Ray Knight. I think now only the latter is still going. By the way I should point out that we didn't like the title of 'Extra' we liked to be known as supporting artists.

The work was spasmodic, you just have to 'check in', with the agency a couple of times a day stating just your name, no conversation as such only if you get asked if you've already been on a particular production. The usual stock answer from the other end is…"Nothing at the moment".

You never knew what you'd get - some good some not so good.

I have always had a fascination for film and the film making process.

The downside of this is the waiting around. For instance you could get called for 7.30 am and you wouldn't be used until late afternoon.

In 9 years or so, I've worked on several TV shows and some major movies.

Some that come to mind are: 'Minder,' 'London's Burning,' 'Soldier, Soldier,' 'The Politician's Wife.'

As well as 'Kavanagh QC,' 'The Maureen Lipman Show,' 'Harry Enfield Show'... and many more.

One TV show was 'Gone to Seed.' I was just pushing a wheelbarrow in this scene and while we were waiting for the crew to set up I asked one of the Assistant Directors, who were the leads in this production and he said Alison Steadman, Jim Broadbent, Peter Cook and Warren Clarke.

As Jim came on the set he came over to me to say hello. We were buddies from the 'Fosdyke Saga' days and we were on the road for four months. It was a pleasant surprise.

Jim introduced me to another actor called Cliff Parisi who had to sit behind a drum kit in this scene and just tap a couple of beats before he said his dialogue.

Jim told him I was a drummer and I jokingly said, 'Let me know if you needs few tips.'

At the end of the shoot I said goodbye to Jim and went home.

The next day I got a phone call from the agency which is quite unusual as they very rarely ring you - generally you have to ring them, anyway, they said that I was called back on 'Gone to Seed,' so I thought that they must have scrapped the scene that we did yesterday and they were doing it again.

I was wrong. They said no, they wanted me as technical adviser for the drum-kit to tune it and make sure it was set up properly. So I did a couple of days on it again.

All the crew and the cameraman, asking if the kit could be moved over a bit and little things to make the shot more accessible and little things like that, treated me completely different.

That's when Jim came over to me and said with a smile, 'I had a word.' Also the money was a bit better as a consultant.

Cheers Jim!

Here are some of the movies that I worked on:

**'Henry V'** directed by Kenneth Branagh.

I was one of the peasants looting the dead bodies after the battle. The whole scene was so moving there was black smoke (half a lorry tyre), white smoke (huge pipes hidden in bushes), plastic horses for the dead ones, as well as real ones with experienced handlers getting them to fall on cue.

And to add more atmosphere to the scene they played an operatic aria over a speaker mounted on the camera platform which was on a dolly, to enable this amazing long tracking shot which stops as Kenneth Branagh gives the famous speech: "Once more unto the breech, dear friends once more".

Very moving.

**'Chaplin'** directed by Lord Richard Attenborough - I was on that for two weeks.

I remember there was a baby grand piano that was used in an earlier scene but was now on the side, off set and earlier Robert Downey Jr was tinkling on it.

Later on while they were setting up the next shot, I went over to it and just tinkled gently,

when I saw Lord Richard walking towards me. So I stood up and started to close the lid, expecting him to tell me off. So I said sorry and he said, 'Not at all, you're ok for a while, we are not set up yet.'

He came across as a genuine nice guy.

Let me just explain how Lord Richard worked.

The first assistant director who is his right hand man sets up a scene while Lord Richard goes to his office. Then when they have all the lighting right and the sound guys are happy and all are set, Lord Richard would come out and take over.

Later on, they were ready to shoot this scene of a bunch of us in evening suits, standing around chatting and we were told to ignore Chaplin as he was wheeled in this wheelchair.

Earlier when they were setting the scene up we were told where to stand and what to do in the scene. Well, we were told to just stand there until Chaplin was wheeled in.
That's what the first Assistant Director told us.
Then Lord Richard comes on the set to direct the scene and he says to me,
"No love...walk into the shot." Well!! I was just about to say, "But he told me to just stand there", but I stopped myself in time. So I did exactly that - I walked into the shot - after all he was the Director and what he says goes. Respect.

I did a day's filming in Borough Market on a movie called **'Blue Ice.'** Michael Caine produced it as well as starring in it, alongside Sean Young (The stunning looking actress in 'Blade Runner'). After Borough Market we all moved to the next location, which was in Hoxton. The back streets where we filmed were dressed to look like Soho.
Michael Caine's character owned a Jazz club and in this scene he arrives at his club in mid-afternoon with his lady and just as he parks his car there's this huge bomb blast which blows off the doors of his club.(I know what you're thinking that was another movie) The blast was done so well that it actually shattered a couple of windows in the neighbouring offices. No one was hurt at all and we were all supplied with ear- plugs because it was so loud. The finished film wasn't all that special, really.

While doing this work, I was fortunate enough to meet and work on the films of two of my favourite people. One was: Jerry Lewis in 'Funny Bones.' I was just a man in the audience dressed in a white suit and a big Stetson. That particular scene was supposed to be in a Las Vegas Cabaret room; we shot it in Ilford! (Ah! the magic of the movies).

In between takes Jerry would walk past me and jokingly make a remark saying something like, 'You'd make a good Hood Ornament.' Translated into English it meant the emblem on a car bonnet. (that gag didn't quite translate)...he was referring to the stupid suit, and the huge hat I was made to wear. That scene took almost the whole day to shoot.

The other major star was Robert De Niro and the film was Mary Shelly's 'Frankenstein' directed by Kenneth Branagh. I worked on that for 9 days. It was bitterly cold as I remember.
I used to have to get the first tube from Caledonia Road Islington to Hammersmith and nip across the road to where a coach was waiting, parked outside The Apollo. The coach left promptly at 6.15am, and took us to Shepperton Studios.
We would all go straight to wardrobe, put on our costumes, (we were Villagers) and they supplied us with long johns, which was a very welcome gesture because it was freezing out on the set, which was built on the grounds, part of which was the car park.
The set was fabulous; a complete village with a market square, a gallows, and huge gates at the end of the village.

For the first three days, De Niro was not in these scenes.
Then on my third day, I was standing at a brazier (they were scattered around, as part of the set, they were real I'm glad to say, lovely and warm), when I saw three people come out of the small building near the set (I later found out that that building was the prosthetics department), and the three people were Robert himself, his girlfriend and his manager. That was my first glimpse of the man. He was wearing green corduroy trousers and sporting a small ponytail.
He had come in for a fitting that day.

He was to play a character who was a patient, and thinks that the doctors are trying to poison him, so he refuses to be inoculated, protests and ends up killing the doctor.

So he goes on the run, but is soon captured and hanged. Later his body is dug up and used for Dr. Frankenstein's experiments, hence the prosthetics for the disfigurement of the face. I'm sure that most people are familiar with the story.

So the next day, we were to shoot the hanging scene. I was one of the baying crowd that gathered to watch; we chatted while we were waiting under the gallows, when we saw this figure coming towards us. We hardly recognised him, he looked really disheveled, hair all over the place. I couldn't believe it was him.

Well-done wardrobe and makeup.

So he climbed onto the gallows, with Kenneth and two men either side of him (one of whom was Jim Carter, who is currently in 'Downton Abbey').

They chatted for a little while, then Branagh stepped down, so we could rehearse the scene.

One of the men put the noose around his neck, while we had to yell, 'Murderer! Murderer! and any other appropriate remark that a crowd would yell in those circumstances.

Then he would yell back at us saying something like 'You are the Murderers. You are the ones that kill people,' and so on. At that point, one of the other men would put a small black sack over his head and they would stop.

We did this a few times, then we went for a 'take.' This was the bit where the makeup women all rushed in and gave the final checks and when they're done they get off the platform.

So, everyone was in their positions - it gets a little tense now as everyone waits for Branagh. He calls 'Action!' and then we start yelling at De Niro. He comes to the edge of the gallows and ...there's a huge pause, (you could see he was getting into the feel of the whole thing). Then he just looked at us and yells, 'F**k you all!' At which point Branagh calls 'Cut!' and he climbs up to the gallows to have a little chat, obviously to tell him to cut out the F**k bit.

All is restored, and we go for another 'take'. This time it was without the first bit, and he went into his speech as rehearsed, and at the end of it, the noose went round his neck and then the black sack, and he was walked to the edge of the platform by the two guards ... and 'Cut.'

That's where the stunt double steps in and picks up from where they stopped, noose round his neck, sack over his head, and he stood at the edge, at which point De Niro comes down and goes to his trailer.

Then - 'Action' and the stunt guy is pushed off the edge for real and just dangles like a rag doll.

It was very dramatic and although he was wearing a harness, it looked so authentic.

The stunt guy did it in about four takes, and on the last one, he actually did hurt his back, I seem to remember. Luckily, it wasn't serious.

The next scene with De Niro was on the following day. He was as the Monster that Frankenstein created. The scene starts with him in this big green cloak, walking through the market, and he steals a loaf of bread from one of the stalls, someone spots him and the chase is on.

We chase him through the square. We're all throwing rocks (polystyrene or some such stuff) at him, at which point he (the monster) picks up this guy and slings him at a fountain in the middle of the square.

At the end of that day's shoot, they gathered us together and asked if anyone could yell out so they could sync. it in later as the guy hits the fountain.

One guy came forward and they counted him in and he let out a scream but it was too high pitched so I volunteered and I let out this mighty yell until it was uncomfortable, but it did the trick 'We'll go with that one,' the sound guy said.

So it's yours truly's voice that's on the movie.

One day there was a helicopter flying around and both De Niro and his stunt double were told to run for cover, as it was the press; they wanted to get some photos of the monster.

We used to have to sign a paper at the end of each day's shooting saying we wouldn't discuss any details about the monsters makeup/look.

When we were chasing the monster he falls into a market stall full of metal jugs and tankards.

It was the stunt double that physically went into them. Again we'd stop after that, and then De Niro would pick up the scene from there, and while they were getting the lighting right, I was right in front waving a big stick and making faces at him and making him laugh, but because he had so much prosthetics on his face he couldn't laugh properly. Most enjoyable.

Here are some other films I worked on: **'Paper Mask,' 'The Rachel Papers,' 'Two Deaths,' 'Great Expectations,' 'Young Indiana Jones,' 'King Ralph,'** and **'The Saint.'**

I was also on **'Splitting Heirs'**, a film written by and starring Eric Idle, and co-starring Barbara Hershey, Rick Moranis and Catherine Zeta Jones. I was head-waiter at this restaurant, attending the table that these people shared.

One couple had a baby with them, which was in one of those baby carriers, and they put it down on the ledge that had some plants on it, behind them while they dined.

Then as they left they forgot the baby.

It wasn't till they got to the disco afterwards that they realised about the baby (a silly plot, or what?). The whole scene was shot in black and white to signify the sixties.

Then they shot another scene at the same restaurant but quite a number of years later when the baby (Eric Idle) was dining with Catherine Zeta Jones.

Because I was in shot at the first bit I got another week's work out of it. This time they greyed my hair to age me a bit.

They also gave Gary Lineker a little cameo part. I had to greet him as he came in to the restaurant.

That was way before his crisps days. I remember he was a little nervous so I told him not to worry as neither of us have any dialogue. I suggested he just go with it. Hasn't he done well since?


I also worked on an episode of a mini-series called **'Centrepoint'** and in this I had to fire a gun. We filmed in Camden under some railway arches.

The guy in charge of the firearms, asked me if I had fired a gun before, so I said jokingly, 'Yes some of the gigs I've done as a drummer you need to use one.' He wasn't amused, I suppose it's because he has a serious job, to make sure everyone is safe when using these things.

So he showed me this handgun and he told me it was the same one that they use in the 'Bond' movies.

I don't know if that's true or just a way of him taking the piss by getting back at me for my earlier gag.

At the point when he started to show me how to hold it etc. the Director came over and said, 'No!! give him this.' It was an 'Uzi'- a sub-machine gun.

So that's what I used. It took a little getting used to because it was so fast. It was obviously firing blanks but it still had a kick to it. The scene was some kind of drug deal that went wrong which turned into a shootout.

Unfortunately the other actor on this scene got a little hurt - nothing too serious.

What happened was we were both hiding behind this stone pillar and firing our guns, and to get the effect of someone shooting back at us the special effects people drill little holes in the stone and put tiny charges and they explode them on cue. Well this poor guy was a little too close to the pillar and he got a couple of small chips of stone that hit him in his face and neck.

He received some medical attention and was sent home. That was the end of the shoot that day.

## IMPROV

There were three improvisation theatre companies that I was involved with.

The first one was called 'The London Theatre Sports.' The best way of describing it is a bit like 'Who's Line Is It Anyway?' where actors play scenes which are totally improvised.

You have two teams, and a referee kitted out just like a football ref, including a whistle round his neck.

The teams challenge each other to various theatre games, for example, they may do a scene where each actor has to start a sentence with a letter suggested by someone in the audience, then the next actor has to answer him or her, starting with the next letter of the alphabet, and so on…until they've used all of the alphabet. I know it doesn't sound that exciting on paper, but believe me it did work. I was playing keyboards for them when they asked the audience for a style of music, then they would make up a song in that given style.

One of my favourite games was called 'Goldfish Bowl.' Let me explain how it works. As the audience are coming into the theatre they're each given a piece of blank paper and a biro and they are asked to write down a sentence and place it in the goldfish bowl on the edge of the stage.

At some point in the show the actors would play a scene, and every now and again they would pull out a piece of paper and read it like, 'I remember what my grandfather used to tell me when I was young. He'd say …' At that point they'd read the suggestion.

The more obscure, the funnier it was.

You can still see them these days at the Comedy Store, in Leicester Square on a Wednesday, or a Sunday, the likes of Paul Merton, Josie Lawrence, Lee Simpson and Richard Vranch (keyboards).

Well worth a visit, but go with an open mind; after all nobody knows exactly how the evening will turn out as it is totally improvised and that's the fun of it.

Another theatre company was The London Playback Company. These actors were a bit more serious. They had a bit of a following.

They would hand out flyers to the audience as they came in, informing them of the 'theme' for that particular week and other themes that were going to be in the coming weeks.

Sad stories, happy stories and so on. Then we would invite a volunteer from the audience to come out front and relate their particular story.

When they had finished they got to choose which actor or actress was to play the characters in their story.

I was on keyboard and supplied the mood music. I got my ideas whilst listening to them relating the story. We had some serious, ones and hilarious ones as well.

The serious ones became a form of therapy for the teller.

I think you've got the gist by now. It certainly kept you on your toes.

I also used to attend improv. classes every Saturday morning, which were more to hone the acting skills really.

There was yet another improv. theatre group.

A very talented Canadian actor Alan Marriott, who was also a voice actor on several productions, 'Bob The Builder' being one of them, led this.

They performed 'Hamlet Improvised. 'It was a condensed version of the Shakespeare play with music added. It was performed in the language it was written in and at certain parts of the play they would ask the audience for a music style and would improvise a song in that style. All very clever stuff.

## THE BOB,CHARLIE & NICK YEARS

Bob Brady and myself gigged together for a number of years. It started in Birmingham after the Old Horns Band faded.

We did a mixture of covers and medleys and one or two of Bob's songs.

The concept worked well considering that we hardly ever rehearsed.

We used to get the crowds joining in and they really got into it. When I moved to London, I shared a basement flat in Notting Hill with Nick Pentelow, then a few months later Bob came down to London and moved in with us.

Three musicians in one tiny flat! The horror!' - but we got on fine.

Pretty soon Bob was gigging in wine bars and one of the first one was Brahms & Liszt (for those who are not familiar with cockney rhyming slang, it means 'pissed') quite an apt name for an establishment that sold alcohol what?

Then later Bob and Nick were doing a few gigs together while I was on the road with various theatrical productions.

Then later when I was free, I joined them.

We three played at one pub off the Edgware Road, near Lords Cricket Ground, called The Crown. It had the nickname of Crocker's Folly, because some chap named Crocker had it built there in 1898. The pub's name was changed to Crocker's Folly and the story was that Frank Crocker built the pub to serve the new terminus of the Great Central Railway, but when the terminus was actually built it was over half a mile away at Marylebone Station, leading to Crocker's ruin, despair and eventual suicide, jumping from the window of an upper floor. That was actually a myth. In reality, Crocker did die in 1904, aged only 41, but of natural causes. It has been claimed that Crocker's ghost haunts the pub.

We played there for a while and at that time it was run by Mick and Vicky and then later by Graham and Ann. By the time the latter were running the pub, this noise control thing came into being. It's a noise regulator and when the decibel levels go up it cuts out the power altogether.

It's the scourge of every musician and as if that wasn't enough there was also the ruling that the landlord needed a special license to have more than two musicians on stage at one time. So in our case Bob who did most of the singing and piano, couldn't really come off so we'd be doing a song. (by the way I was playing congas not the drum kit). Then, when the sax solo came up, I would disappear into the side and Nick would come on do his solo then he would go to the side and I would come on. What a stupid ruling. When you think about it, you could have two loud guitars that would make more noise, than say a string quartet. Bullshit!!

We sometimes had a few guests who would get up and do a couple of numbers. One of these was Frankie Miller. He had a great voice - very gravely and full of soul.

Some of you might remember one of his hits. It was "Darlin ... feeling kind of lonesome." This one time he got up with us and I asked him what song did he fancy and he said 'He'll have to Go,' the old Jim Reeves song. But his version was by far nothing like Jim's thank God. It was raunchy, gutsy and soulful. I think Ry Cooder did a similar version.

Another guy who got up with us now and again was Den Hegarty. He was the deep bass voice in a band called Darts. Once he's on stage he goes mental; he would climb over tables, throw himself into people's laps - you just never knew what he was going to do next, all this while holding a mic and singing. He once climbed into the piano (Baby Grand) and closed the lid on himself while singing 'Blue Moon'…great character.

We gathered quite a following over the years and some of the friends we made back in the 80's we are still in touch with, to this present day.

Great friends all of them: Angela, Pauline, Margaret and Martina.

I guess I'd better stop in case I leave someone out.

The one pub that we played in for the longest period was the Kings Head on Upper Street, Islington, North London.

All in all we were there for about 4 or 5 years.

The atmosphere was electric; everybody joining in, especially when we did 60's medley and a Beatles medley.

'The Blues Brothers' medley always got a great response too, especially 'Rawhide.' I used to do cattle noises and whistle to move the cattle effect.

We used to start the medley with 'Peter Gunn' the instrumental, while I narrated some dialogue from the film.

The Kings Head was also a fringe theatre in the back room.

Lots of performers started there in the years that we played such as: Victoria Wood, French & Saunders, Hugh Grant, Sheila Steafel and Neil Innes, to name a few.

I've seen some great productions there one of which was a musical called 'Mr. Cinders.' The one song that was well known from that show is 'Spread A Little Happiness.' Sting had a hit with it.

All the music for that show was written by a lovely elderly gentleman called Vivian Ellis

Bob and I used to do it in our show, and one night Mr. Ellis was in the audience, and he complimented us on it. They were great days and as I said before, we made lots of friends and we are still in touch.

There was a picture framing shop in Cross Street around the corner from the King's Head, called 'The Frame Factory' and all the staff used to come and see Bob and myself.

There was Jeff, Eric, Angela, Juliet, and Elsa.

Giovanni the hairdresser was next door. Giovanni who liked to be called John, is an Italian/Londoner – a great guy. He and his wife were sharp dressers. Sadly his wife died in her prime.

A couple of years later he opened a place next door to his hairdressing salon and started selling designer men's and women's clothes.

I bought a couple of jackets from there.

Ah! Happy days.

Bob and I did a few gigs with Bob's other half on bass guitar. Her name is Megan Davies. She was with the chart-topping group 'The Applejacks'

She also joined Bob and I in a few New Year's Eve gigs in Kent when I first moved down there.

We also played in a few other pubs in Islington and we met an assortment of characters.

The one thing I learnt there was to never ask anybody what they did for a living.

At the King's Head the theatre was in the back room
and we were in the front so we could not start playing
until the play was over.

It all depended on the length of the particular
production at the time. There was one comedy review
show called 'The Jockeys of Norfolk'. It was three
guys doing a few sketches and one of the guys was
Hugh Grant.

They were quite funny, especially one sketch, where
they took a very English story called 'The Winslow
Boy' and played it as a Martin Scorsese piece, starring
Robert De Niro, Al Pacino and Robert Duval. Very
funny indeed.

Dan Crawford, who was from New York, ran the Kings
Head Theatre. He built it up over the years by putting
on good shows, some of which transferred to the West
End.

Sadly he passed away. I went to his memorial service at
the church right across the road from the Kings Head.

I have some very fond memories from there.

Janice, who was well loved by all the regulars, ran the
front bar. Bob and I met all the performers who worked
there

At one time, we met a Liverpudlian actor/ musician
who was doing a one man show.

He was Carl Chase and the show was about Hank
Williams, the Country &Western singer-songwriter of
such hits like: 'Your Cheating Heart' and 'Lonesome
Me.' The show was called: 'Hank Williams, The Show
He Never Gave' ... and just after that, he got a part in
the first Batman movie as one of the Joker's (Jack
Nicholson's) men.

We got on well with Carl; he was a down to earth type
of guy - definitely not a 'luvvie!'

One day he told me this little story about working with
Jack.

Carl said that he had a small part in a film called 'Distance Voices, Still Lives' back in '88' and the film was shown on TV one night and Jack had watched it. Carl said that Jack told him that he watched it last night in his hotel, and he thought that he was very good in it. Carl said to me, 'I was flattered to get a compliment, from someone of his stature.'

He continued, 'I was lost for words; I mean what do you say to that, so I came out with, "Thanks! I think I've seen you in something or other recently." He said they both had a laugh about it.

A few weeks before each Christmas, it was decorations time.

The routine was as follows: We regulars would wait until all the other punters left the pub then we would stay behind.

Janice would then send a couple of the staff upstairs to get the decorations and ladders and we would designate someone to be on cocktail duty.

The pub has a very high ceiling, hence the ladders. The whole thing was fun and we'd obviously stop now and again to make use of the cocktails.

We would be there till dawn by which time the Maltese cafe next door would open and we would go for breakfast.

The one thing that was different about the Kings Head was that it was the only pub in London that did not change to decimalisation; although you got your change in decimal currency, the till was the old style with, pounds, shillings and pence. So you'd buy a couple of drinks and the barman/woman would say, 'Twelve shillings and sixpence please.' It used to freak people out if they had never been there before.

One day I walked in to the Kings Head at lunchtime, and as soon as I went to the bar the person behind the bar said that someone from the office wanted to talk to me. The office was upstairs, it was the administration office for the theatre. When I got there one of the staff gave me a piece of paper with an address in New Cross, South London.

She told me that Gary Oldman was interviewing actors for a film, which he had written and was going to direct. He was not going to be acting in it, just directing. The film was 'Nil by Mouth,' and he was looking for a singer in a pub scene. I thanked her and made my way over there.

I eventually found the building; it was some kind of community centre. I walked up one flight of stairs and there was only one door up there. I knocked..."Come in". So, in I went and Gary was sitting behind a desk with lots of paper and a couple of photos on it.

We shook hands. I was totally in awe of this guy. I think he ranks as one of Britain's greatest actors.

We talked about my background, music and the few acting things that I had done, then he explained a bit about the film.

He wanted someone in a pub who gets up and sings with the musicians. He also added that it was still just an idea and not set in concrete. After about forty-five minutes or so we said our goodbyes and I left.

I guess that when you've been in showbiz for a long time you learn not to see anything as a certainty until you're actually doing it and even then it may not be used.

Even so, it was nice to meet the guy.

Although I haven't seen the film, I heard that he used an actress to play his mum and she is the person that gets up and sings.

There was group in Islington called 'The Raving Jeckylls'. Let me explain the word Jeckyll. In cockney slang, if something is Jeckyll its dodgy, Jeckyll and Hyde = snide, something that's snide is dodgy, you get the idea.

Bob and I learned a lot of cockney slang and each time we heard a new one, we'd ask someone what it meant. A quick short list: Money: £1= Sovereign or Sov for short. 2, Bottle…Bottle of glue = 2. 3, 30 or 300 a carpet ( the way it was explained to us was when you've done three years in prison you're entitled to a small carpet in your cell). I don't know if that's true or not. 4 is a rouf four backwards, 5 is a Jacks Alive, or just Jacks, 6 is half a stretch, a stretch in prison is 12 months so… 7 is a neves seven backwards,
8 and 9 I don't know, it's not slang, I really don't know. 10, Cockle and Hen,…12 a stretch, as explained earlier. Then we go up to 20 Apple - apple core = score, 25 a pony…no idea why.100 a ton. £500… a monkey.
I could go on, but you get the gist, or perhaps you've lost the will to live by now.
As I was saying the Raving Jeckylls were playing at a pub in Kingsland Road called The Nice Little Earner, (no, I'm not making it up).
This particular Sunday evening it was Letitia Dean's 21st Birthday, (Letitia is an actress in East Enders) , and the Jeckylls were playing there. The pub was closed to the public.
I was invited because Mandy the Manageress at the pub, who was a very good friend of Letitia invited me, plus I'd already met Letitia at Gerry's club the watering hole in Soho.
There were quite a few of the cast of 'East Enders' there.
I had been there for about thirty minutes when the drummer offered me his seat; in other words he motioned for me to sit in with the band. I've never been known to turn down a chance to play.
I got up and we started playing some Motown number. Can't remember which.
During this number in walked Anita Dobson, another one of the cast, with her was her husband, Brian May,

one hell of a guitarist (Queen). They both went to the bar after Letitia greeted them.

As we finished the second number, Brian May made his way towards the guitarist and it looked as if he was going to get up with the band. At that point I signalled to the drummer to see if he wanted to get back on his drums, but he signalled back telling me to stay.

And with that, we started playing a slow blues, with the great Brian May.

Well, it goes without saying, he was magic.

We did one of those endings where the drummer and guitar battle it out to finish last. I'm not saying who did but it was great.

Shortly after that I handed back to the drummer and I went back to the bar.


Bob and I played at many an East End pub, some good some not so good. You used to get these characters in these places like one guy who got up to sing. He was a sharp dresser, wearing lots of tom (tomfoolery = jewellery).

So we asked him what he was going to sing and he replied, 'My Way'… same key as Frank!'

Bob and I looked at each other and we said what key is that then and he said, 'B' flat. So Bob started the introduction and it was, 'And Now…And Now…And Now'…till eventually he got his pitch, somewhere near right, and got on with it. But of course in these cases the friends of the person who gets up to sing have a tendency to blame the musicians, saying that we weren't  good enough to back them.

Another thing that never ceases to amuse me is…when they come up to me on the drums and tell me what song they're going to do …I'll let that sink in for a bit…

OK, I don't determine the key of the song or indeed, whether I know it or not, I can always lay the beat, no problem.

In other words, speak to the pianist, not me!

# CARUANA

I'm a great believer in coincidences. Let me explain one:

I got married way back in '73. We went to Malta for the honeymoon which was the first time that I had visited Malta since leaving in '55.

We had a good time. We went around the island and did the usual touristy things etc.

One night we went to St Paul's Bay, an area very popular with English holidaymakers and there was a restaurant there called Palazzo Pescatori. Fabulous place - excellent food and as the name states they specialise in a variety of fish.

On this particular night there was a pianist backing a male singer. He was singing standards by 'Sinatra', 'Tony Bennett' etc… he had a good voice, and when he spoke between numbers it sounded as if he came from London.

Anyway, when he came off for his break we were at the bar and I offered him a drink and we got talking  By this time I was convinced the he was English.

We both told him that we enjoyed his singing and he went back on stage. It turns out that he was Maltese, but he, like me had lived in the UK for a long time. Now I know by now you're thinking, "When is he going to get to the point?" Patience my friend.

Now let's reel on to a considerable number of years later, (way after the divorce and the Wizzard days as well), to where I'm living in London.

The time when I'm doing gigs with Bob Brady in Islington.

One particular pub was The Edward VII, and one night after we finished playing we were chatting to the regulars, one of them started talking about this Italian singer called Ray Caron who does the East- End pub circuit. We hadn't come across him. They continued to say that he had represented the UK in the Eurovision Song Contest.

Then one night I went to Stringfellow's (this was way before it became a lap dancing club) and I went downstairs to the disco floor. It was packed solid, so I just stayed on the stairs. Then out of the crowd this guy was coming up the stairs; as he got level with me he looked at me and said, 'Hello mate I know you from somewhere don't I?' We both threw in a few suggestions as to where we knew each other from, then eventually we came to the same answer: Malta

That's when I recognised him as being the guy that sang in the Palazzo Pescatore, back in Malta over twenty odd years ago. So we chatted over a couple of drinks. I asked him what he was up to and he told me that he was doing East-End pubs, and the odd private do.

I asked him what name he went under and he said Ray Caron. His real name is Ray Caruana but Caron is much easier for the punters to pronounce.

So here's the very same guy that the guys at the Edward VII were talking about.

Much later when I started doing gigs on my own on piano/vocals, I used to bump into him at certain gigs like: The Blue Last, in Shoreditch and The Brownlow Arms, near the Hackney Road. As well as his singing he is an accomplished leather craftsman. I think he's doing more of the latter now.

Just a few lines about my first visit to 'Stringfellow's'. Bob and I were invited to go with some of the guys from the Islington pub. They said they were members and knew Peter Stringfellow personally and that they would introduce us to Peter.

So we went and they got us in but Bob and I stayed in the upstairs bar while the other guys went down to the disco.

After we'd been there quite a while it looked like the guys had forgotten about the introduction. I then said to Bob, 'Sod this, I'm going to find him myself.'

So I went downstairs and almost right away I saw Peter. I introduced myself and told him that I remembered him from the club in Leeds that I had played at in the sixties, where he was a DJ. That broke the ice somewhat and then I told him about the duo and that we were both in the club.

To my utter surprise he said, 'Why don't you guys do a half hour or so upstairs? You must have seen the Baby Grand as you came in.'

'OK,' I said and went upstairs to tell Bob.

Bob looked at me as if I was mad. 'What the hell are you going to play? You haven't got the congas with you.'

'No problem,' I said. And with that I went up to the bar and asked the barman for two empty ice buckets. He looked puzzled, but then I told him that Peter said it was OK. So he handed two ice buckets over to me. At that point Peter had come upstairs and came towards the bar. I introduced him to Bob and he said that he'd get someone to make sure the microphone was on and get a spare one for my 'buckets.'

That's all it took, honest. We started with a boogie instrumental then Bob went into a couple of Rock' n' Roll vocal numbers and by the second vocal number the crowd started taking notice - all those rich city types were getting into it. Meanwhile I was struggling to keep these ice buckets firmly between my legs. I hadn't realised until after, that the metal of the buckets was making black marks on my white trousers, not to mention my hands were killing me.

'Oh how we suffer for our art!' Somebody must have said that, if not, then I just did.

Anyway, we went down pretty well.

Then afterwards Peter bought us a drink and introduced us to Peter Stockton, one of his managers, to arrange a couple of gigs. By the way, I did explain to Peter that I did have congas and wouldn't be using his buckets. We had a laugh about it. So that's how we got our first gig at Stringfellow's.

Then we were booked for special events like his birthday in October, the club's birthday in August, but the only way we got these gigs was through me going in from time to time and having a drink with Peter. He would just say something like, 'You guys are playing at my birthday next week aren't you? Go and see Peter and get it booked in.'

One night when we were playing there I was playing away with my eyes closed as you do and I sensed that there was another person tapping on my congas, and when I opened them this huge face was staring at me and smiling. It was Joe Frazier, the boxer.

What you gonna do, tell him to piss off? He was cool, because he then got up on stage with us and sang some Tamla Motown song with us. I think it was 'Stand by Me.'

## R.L.S.B

In 1988 I had a mild heart attack. I was in Whittington Hospital North London for about 12 days.

When I came out I was very kindly looked after by Annie the florist and her family for a couple of weeks. I am eternally grateful for their kindness.

My old friend Gary Whelan, (Irish actor) had organised a fundraising event at an Irish bar called Minogues, which was run by another dear friend of mine, Ethel Minogue.

I attended the 'do' but I was on strict instructions not to even think of getting on the drums. There was a band playing and my old mate Luddy Samms, a fine soul singer, fronted it. He was originally from Brum.

There were about two to three hundred people there and it was very humbling to see such a turn out.

Altogether it was a very nice gesture from everyone concerned to do this for me.

Later Gary told me that he had got in touch with Bob Hoskins, to ask him to come, but unfortunately he was working away somewhere.

Months later I saw Bob Hoskins in Belsize Park Road, he was shopping at his favourite greengrocers on the high street.

We said hello and he apologised for not coming to the do.

He said, "Are you ok? I heard you were dying".

I replied jokingly "It's okay for some people, I have a heart attack and I'm out of work, you have a heart attack and you get paid for it."

I was referring to the fact that he had just done a film recently with Denzel Washington, and the gist of the story was: Bob's character was always eating burgers and fast food and has a heart attack. The film was called 'Heart Condition.'

Bob played a racist cop who receives a heart transplant from a black lawyer he hates, who returns as a ghost to ask the cop to help take down the men who murdered him. We both had a giggle about it.


A couple of months later while I was taking things easy, a pal of mine Ivan Cox, artist and sculptor, asked me if I was strong enough to do a bit of teaching to a group of kids who are blind or partially sighted.

The school is called Dorton House and it's down in Kent, in a little place called Seal, near Sevenoaks.

The school comes under the umbrella of The Royal London Society for the Blind.

Ivan was teaching art and woodwork there about three days a week.

I said I would give it a go and he said it would probably be just a couple of hours a week.

So he arranged a meeting for me with the Principal and I went down one day.

Mr. Talbot was a pleasant chap. We talked for a while and I told him that I'd never taught before and certainly not special needs children.

We chatted for a bit longer and we agreed to give it a try for three hours one day a week starting the coming Tuesday.

There was only three weeks before they would break up for Easter, so we'd use those three weeks to see if the kids enjoyed the lessons (actually, the word 'lessons' was probably wrong - it was more like therapy). They enjoyed it and I tried to make it as much fun as I could.

After the Easter holiday I went back down to find out whether they wanted me to continue and the answer was yes.

The next thing I know, I had been there for five years. I was still doing the odd film extra thing when I could. There was a college being built on the campus and in 1989 Her Majesty the Queen came to open the college.

Shortly after that the film work was coming in more often and I was having to go for castings for commercials, therefore it all started clashing with the regular Tuesdays and rather than keep messing them about I decided to stop for a while.

I kept in touch with a couple of the staff though.

Much later I got in touch with Jo Glazier who worked at the college. We just chatted about the kids and just caught up on the news in general and she suggested that I ought to visit.

So I did just that. I went down one day and saw Jo. She was now in 'Mobility', working with a team of people who taught the kids how to get around using their cane, although of course there was more to it than that.

It's a very highly skilled and responsible job. They train them to get around not just around the campus, but they also take them into the village and town centre where they have to deal with traffic, other people, obstacles, noise etc.

It's a very harrowing experience for the kids dealing with these things.

Jo introduced me to Brian Cooney who is the Principal at college, and we chatted for a while. He asked me about my background and experience in working with visually impaired students then he asked me if I would be prepared to start teaching drumming again. I told him I'd think about it for a couple of days and get back to him.

Well I gave it some thought and a few days later I decided that I would do it again.

So I went back down to Kent and I started teaching again. This time there was a mixture of ages of the kids.

I also did Summer School, which included kids with similar disabilities as our own kids. It was more relaxed than ordinary school. I'm sure you all know what summer school is. We all had fun.

I remember one particular teenager; he was totally blind and deaf. He had a woman with him who talked to him using her hand on his left hand. Fascinating to watch - she was so quick. We were taught the deaf /blind alphabet, but it took a lot of practice and we were a lot slower than her.

I asked her what activity he would like to do and he told her, 'drumming. My first thought was, how do you go about teaching a deaf and blind person to play drums?

But I was pleasantly surprised as I got there in the end. I tapped his knee for the bass drum and guided his hands for the snare and hi hat. I was amazed; it only took him a couple of minutes to master it and off he went.

It took me longer to stop myself from talking instructions to him. He had natural rhythm as we saw when we had a disco at the end of the week and he was dancing really well. The lady with him told me he felt the vibrations.

I found it all absolutely amazing.

One summer we had an adult student coming over from Bethlehem who was visually impaired but not totally blind. He wanted to train as a music therapist, but the college couldn't provide such a course. We managed to get him on a preliminary course with Nordorf Robbins in Kentish Town in London.

So I was appointed to escort him up to London and back once a week and write down anything that was needed.

For the rest of the week I was a classroom assistant as well as the drum tutor, so it felt like a proper day job really.

Eventually I moved from London and went to live in Kent, on campus actually.

Altogether I was there for fifteen years.

Over the years I gave drum and piano/keyboard lessons, worked with music technology recording on computer and I also organised quite a few fundraising events in and around the Sevenoaks area.

Every summer just before they broke up for the holidays we used to put on a concert, featuring the kids. We called it 'Star for a Night' and the kids thoroughly enjoyed it right from the rehearsals, leading up to the night of the actual performance.

It was a chance for them to perform in front of an audience and their families. They were very professional.

Altogether a talented bunch.

The other fundraising productions that I got together were a couple of 'Variety Nights' in which I called on some of my performing friends. People like, 'Isosceles', two very funny comedians/actors, who have a unique act, and they involve the audience in their act. Altogether they are crowd pleasers. Then there's Richard McDougall, a superb magician with a slick act of magic and humour.

Then there were musicians, who helped me out by giving their time for free, they were:
Bob Brady (keyboard and vocals), Megan Davies, (bass and vocals), Nick Pentelow (sax and flute) as well as The Jive Aces, a superb jive band and very entertaining, and a dance troupe called 'The Jiving Lindy hoppers.'
I used to get a great deal of satisfaction working with these kids. I reckon I learned as much from them as they did from me.
There were too many to mention them all but here's a few of them: Andrew Bourne (born without eyes), Little Daisy (the same), Guy (Batten's Disease); he loved bands like 'Free,' 'Queen,' 'Deep Purple,' and one of his favourite songs by Free is 'Wishing Well' which he used to play on the piano and we both would sing it.
Not many people have heard of Batten's disease, so here is a brief description:
Batten's disease is a fatal, inherited disorder of the nervous system that typically begins in childhood. Early symptoms of this disorder usually appear between the ages of 5 and 10 years, when parents or physicians may notice a previously normal child has begun to develop vision problems or seizures. In some cases the early signs are subtle, taking the form of personality and behaviour changes, slow learning, clumsiness, or stumbling. Over time, affected children suffer mental impairment, worsening seizures, and progressive loss of sight and motor skills. Eventually, children with Batten disease become blind, bedridden,

and demented. Batten disease is often fatal by the late teens or twenties.

One early December I was driving along a narrow country lane and as I approached this one particular corner there was another car coming the opposite way and we went straight into each other. My main injury was my left ankle and I was in hospital for about a week. When I came out, Karrie, who is Mike Curd's wife, picked me up.
They very kindly put me up for a few days in their spare room.
I was in plaster for a considerable time.
I first met Mike and Karrie when I moved down to Kent from London. Mike is a very accomplished freelance TV and film editor. He's also a whizz on Mac computers and has helped me with my iMac many times. They invited me to Sunday lunch on several occasions. For a few years they both ran The Chequers pub in Heaverham. I had some lovely New Year's Eves there. Bob Brady and his other half, Megan, and I played for them on quite a few occasions. Good times.
I have to say that Karrie did a magnificent job of running the pub. The atmosphere was always pleasant and relaxing.
The pub has had many other landlords since but it's the times of Karrie and Mike that people remember best. Since they came out of the pub, it hasn't been the same.
Whilst using the pub I made a few friends there; people like Tony and Hazel. Tony always encouraged me to write a book. He loved the little anecdotes that I subjected him to on many an occasion.
There was also Lyn and Lindsey, a lovely couple. Lyn used to work with the little ones at Dorton School for the Blind and Lindsey used to be a TV newsreader and broadcaster.
The village of Kemsing is really my manor so to speak and I know everyone there and vice versa.

As I said before I've made a lot of friends whilst living in Kent

Another couple who I was introduced to at the early stages of my moving down, was Nick and his lovely wife Lesley. I first met them through Jo Wooltorton who was the art teacher at Dorton House School. It was at a birthday party at their house in Edenbridge. We've become good friends over the years. They're a lovely couple and they're also blessed with lovely grown up children.


There was one student from the earlier days of when I first started there and he was Melvin.

Melvin is a very talented person - he plays piano, bass, sings, writes songs and he has perfect pitch, good going for someone who has no vision at all.

One day he said to me, 'Do you like Country and Western music, Mr. Grima?' I soon stopped him using 'Mr. Grima'.

I told him to call me Charlie.

It went against the usual school's protocol,but I didn't believe in all that.

'Yes I do like some of it. Why do you ask?' I replied.

'Well' he said, 'I listen to someone who you've probably never heard of.

'Try me,' I said.

'I listen to Raymond Froggatt,' he said. 'I love his songs.'

So I told him that I knew Raymond very well, or 'Froggie' as us Brummie musicians affectionately call him.

I've known him for years; I was in his band for a few months and I socialised with him and Hartley Kane his long- time guitarist.

Well his face was a picture; he was so pleased.

From then on he used to ask me if I'd been to Birmingham lately and have I seen Raymond?

This went on for a few weeks. Then one weekend while I was in Birmingham, I managed to contact Hartley Kane and asked him if he was going to be seeing Raymond soon.

'He's right here in my place,' he said. 'Do you want to talk to him?' So any way I explained the Melvin scenario to him and he told me to come over and see them both.

So I jumped on the next train to Telford.

They took a little break from their rehearsing and we all had a good old chinwag.

I explained in more detail about Melvin being totally blind and that he was a great fan of theirs and then I asked if there was a chance of a cassette for Melvin and Froggie gave me two cassettes and an LP (we're talking vinyl here). I told them that Melvin would be over the moon about that.

So the following week before Melvin came for his usual session I had someone braille a message on the LP cover.

When Melvin came in I didn't say anything about my Birmingham trip.

We just got on with the session, (I call it that because it wasn't a lesson as such more of a fun session).

So when we finished and he was about to go I said, 'Melvin, someone left this LP in here and it's got braille writing on it. Can you tell me who it is?'

As his fingers began to read I was watching his face he began: "To Melvin, very best wishes, from Raymond Froggatt. Keep writing your songs and good luck for the future."

Well he couldn't get his breath...then I gave him the two cassettes and he said, 'How much do I have to pay for these?' I told him they were all presents from 'Froggie.'

It still brings a lump to my throat when I tell this story. So for the next few weeks he played and sang Froggie's songs in his session with me.

It's moments like these that stay with you.

Then there was Sam - he was eight years old, totally
blind, with an amazing feel for music.
The first time that he came to me for his lesson I had
just learned the instrumental bit of Eric Clapton's
'Layla' and I played it to him. He sat there listening then
(I swear this is true) he got on the piano and started
playing it. Yes there were a couple of notes not quite
right, but hey, he had never heard the tune before
I was stunned! What an absolutely talented little kid.

I mentioned before that I was involved in a few
fundraising ventures for the Society and here's a couple
of them: We were in touch with the society for the
blind in Sicily and an exchange trip was set up for a
few of our kids who would visit there first then at a
later date we would play host to the Italians when they
come to us.
To raise funds the kids/students did a few money-
raising things themselves like sponsored swimming, car
washing and so on...
At the time I was living in Islington and I used to
frequent an Italian restaurant on Upper Street. The
owner was a Sicilian so I asked him if I could organise
a fund raising evening in his restaurant. He eventually
agreed.
So I rang Bob Brady, Nick Pentelow, and Megan
Davies, who all said yes straight away. That was the
music taken care off. Now for some magic. I rang
Richard McDougall an absolutely superb performer and
a friend.
He said yes too not only that but on the night he
brought another magician with him and they did close
up magic at the tables. The deal was a three-course
dinner and the entertainment. The food was first class
and so was the entertainment. In the interval there was
a mini auction.

I was going to do it but Eddie McPherson an old friend of mine from Gerry's Club said she would do the auction. In her own words, 'You know everybody here and you won't get as much money as if I do it.' So I didn't argue.

She did a great job, a lot better than if I'd done it. Eddie is the mother of Graham McPherson better known as 'Suggs' from Madness – a great guy.

All in all the night was very successful and we raised a little over a thousand pounds towards the Sicily trip.

I went on the trip with them. We flew to Catania where we would be based, and Mount Etna was about 40 odd kilometres from there.

The following day we went to Etna in a hired coach which takes you to the base then we all had to transfer to this high military looking, four wheel drive vehicle which seated 6 to 8 people.

That takes you to another level where we got out and onto a cable car to yet another level and as you're going up you look down and can see the houses below. Well actually, just the roofs and chimneys - the rest was buried in this dark grey dust.

Now we asked the kids, who wanted to go to the top? Only about 3 said yes and there was enough staff to cope with all the kids so I stayed in the shop.

The top level is quite high and I was getting breathless at this one, after all I was the oldest of all the staff. It is strange to see snow on the ground, and in places there were little cracks in the ground where you could see the red hot lava underneath. There was also a very strong smell of sulphur.

Altogether our stay in Sicily was not long enough. We were looked after very well and there was no language barrier at all, everyone spoke English.

When it came to meal times, our students found it strange to cope with the amount of food that was served, for instance a big plate of spaghetti would come and our kids thought that was it but no, that was just the starter, then the pesce spade (swordfish) would arrive; only a few managed both courses. Of course I was in my element; it was just like back home in Malta where pesce spada was one of my favourite fish.

A month or so after we got back it was our turn to play the hosts to the Italians. They had a good time with us. We tried to match their hospitality. They wanted to taste fish and chips, so we arranged to take them to Hastings - not quite the blue of the Mediterranean but it didn't matter, they enjoyed themselves.

There were many feel-good moments like this over the fifteen years or so that I worked there.

It humbles you when you stop to think about how they all cope with complete blindness and visual impairment.

So next time you see someone with a white cane, spare a thought.

## ISAAC

Isaac is remarkable chap who worked at Dorton House School in IT.

He is a great character with a wonderful sense of humour.

He is from Kenya and he's totally blind.

When I first moved down from London I was sleeping in a little room on campus. Isaac had a flat on campus as well.

After a few months he moved out of his place on campus and rented a small two bedroom house in a little village called Noah's Ark (honest). The reason for the move was because his girlfriend was coming over from America to join him, but not for six months or so. So he rented me the other room on a short -term basis. This house was so not blind person friendly at all. First of all there were three steps down from the lane to the front door, then you went through the front room and down three steps again to the kitchen. The stairs to the bedrooms were very steep and you had to go through my room to the bathroom, wait for it, down more steps, and you had to duck because of the low ceiling.

I helped him move in with one of the school's vans. As we were moving his stuff in he turned to me and said, 'Charlie, is there a cat in here?' So I started sniffing for a tomcat's pee smell.

'I can't smell anything.' I said.

'No.' He said. 'I can hear one.' Sure enough there was this next-door neighbour's black cat, which wandered in to say hello I guess. That's when we both fell about laughing. He is totally blind and I have a hearing impairment. We were both reminded of the Richard Pryor and Gene Wilder movie 'See no Evil, Hear no Evil.' When I eventually moved in we used to get those moments all the time. For instance, he had a TV with a huge screen and he used to have the volume quite low. Well, I could see the movie or programme but couldn't hear a bloody thing, but I didn't complain, after all it was his telly.

Because he had a great sense of humour we had a good laugh. In the morning when the post came he would sometimes pick it up and pretend to look through it and I used to say, 'Anything for me Isaac?' To which he replied, 'No it's all for me, sorry.' And after we had a laugh, I would look at the post and if there was an official looking envelope he would ask me to open it for him and read it to him.

He had a stock of jokes like he would say... 'I had a nightmare last night. I dreamt I got my eyesight back.' The first time I heard it I said, 'Why is that a nightmare?'

'Well!! Because I lost all my benefits.'

One day I was at the reception at the college and as he came walking past me the only word he heard me say to the receptionist was, 'Thanks.'

'Hi Charlie,' he said and carried on up the corridor.

So I caught up with him and said, 'How did you know it was me from just one word?'

To which he replied, 'Oh!! It's just a black thing, man.'
As I said earlier, he's a remarkable person.

He was born with sight then when he was 15/16 he
suffered an illness, which gradually got worse until it
developed to total blindness.

During my time at Dorton I got more and more into
computers. I have an iMac (three in fact, three different
generations). I wanted to get more into them and after
downloading a few tutorials I had a go at creating my
own website. It was pretty difficult at first but I
persevered and finally it paid off. The trouble is,
technology is always changing and it's hard to keep up
with the latest software.

So what I'm trying to say is, my website needs
updating.


As I have an e-mail facility on there I get e-mails from
people some of whom I've never heard of.

One such person is Eric Montfort, a Maltese DJ and
journalist for a Mediterranean radio station who is very
knowledgeable about bands and songwriters etc.

He e-mailed me to ask if he could interview me over
the phone then he would broadcast it later on his show.
I agreed and it went well considering that I wasn't fully
awake when he rang.

Most of the questions, as you might have guessed, were
about my time with Wizzard.

He also touched on my Birmingham background and
went on to the bands at that time, in fact the whole
Brum music scene.

He had done his research well, because he knew every
musician that I mentioned.

People like Steve Gibbons, Raymond Froggatt, Jeff
Lynne, Ozzy and many more.

He told me that I was the only Maltese musician to
have been involved with a band that had two No1 hits.

When I went to Malta in 2013, I met up with him and we went to the radio station where I was interviewed again, this time by one of the other DJs.

A bigger than life guy called Martin Sapiano, he was very animated and quite energetic. He played a couple of Wizzard songs in between the interview.

Recently Eric came to the UK to do some interviews with a couple of artistes. I think Alice Copper was one of them. He stayed in Eastbourne at another Maltese musician's place.

That musician is Tony Carr the only other Maltese percussionist that I know. Tony is retired now. He's 86 and he was a session drummer/percussionist in the '70's. He was in Alan Price's band and he's done loads of sessions with people like Donovan, Duran Duran and many more.

It was nice to catch up with him because I had met him very briefly in the 70's in George Martin's Air Studios in Oxford Circus, but we never kept in touch.

We had a good old chinwag about all the sessions and musicians that we both knew.

A couple of years ago I went through a triple heart bypass operation.(I bet you didn't know that I had 3 hearts did you?)

So subsequently I retired.

I now do the occasional voluntary bit of teaching of drums & keyboards.

I like to encourage young students to appreciate good music. There are quite a lot of talented kids around.

I do a bit of home recording just as a hobby, and I still enjoy designing interiors, on my computer.

I hope you've enjoyed some of the stories in this book. Here are a few Limericks, as a reward for your patience in hearing me waffling on about me…Enjoy!!!

# LIMERICKS

## SHEEP

If people count sheep to sleep
What method is used by the sheep?
Do they count horses, chickens, or pigs
Or do they count effigies of Little Bo Peep?

## MY AGENT

'There's not much at the moment,' my agent said to me
As he came out bloody legless from the bar at the BBC
I don't like it when he goes on these benders
So far all he's ever got me is a walk-on on
'Eastenders.'

## VINCENT VAN GOGH

Van Gogh went downtown for a beer
Which he found exceedingly dear
When in walked his brother
And offered Vincent another
And Vince said, 'No thanks, I've one 'ere.'

## MUSICIAN

A young musician named Cyril
Whose face resembled a squirrel
Played a gig down in Kent
Just to help pay his rent
Then he drove all the way home to the Wirral.

## MOZART

Mozart recorded a recital
But he left out a few notes, which were vital
His manager said, 'Son, what's done is done
Don't worry we'll just change the title.'

## THE BARD

If Shakespeare was writing today
He would use a computer I'd say

He would surf on 'The Net'
And I'm willing to bet
That 'All's Well' at the end of the day.

## MAGICIANS

I do think Magicians are clever
Producing rabbits from hats
But how come though they're good, do they never
Do something fancy with cats.

## MICHAELANGELO

As artistic achievements go
Think of Michaelangelo
I mean we all know that feeling
When it comes to painting a ceiling
We've all got a long way to go.

## DA VINCI

DaVinci was one hell of a geyser
To come up with that gem 'Mona Lisa'
He painted with style
And gave her that smile
That makes you just want to squeeze her.

## VIGO

(veego)
An Italian student named Vigo
Claimed that studying 'Karl Marx' boosts the ego
He asked what I thought
With my conscience I fought
But I still prefer, 'Groucho',' Harpo' and 'Chico.'

## G.B.S

He criticised most plays that he saw
But his own plays were of course without flaw
Like 'Arms and the Man'
And Pygmalion
That man was George Bernard Shaw.

## CLINT

Clint Eastwood was expected to pay
His ex-girlfriend millions they say
But her lawyer was praying
He'd not hear Clint saying
'Go ahead punk, make my day.'

## ACTOR

There was a young actor from Rhyl
Who landed a part on 'The Bill'
He played a young copper
Who arrested a shopper
Who was caught with his hand in the till.

## ARCHIE

A concert pianist named Archie
Played a real 'Bum gig' in Karachi
His agent Felicity said, 'What you need's more
publicity,'
And with that she phoned Saatchi & Saatchi.

## DALI

Sometimes Dali paints in his socks
While drinking Scotch on the rocks
Then he'll have another
And another and another
That accounts for his old drooping clocks.

## MARY SHELLY'S FRANKENSTEIN

Branagh asked De Niro to tea
To discuss Frankenstein and Rob's fee
Then after quite a long time
Rob gave Kenneth a smile
And replied, 'Are you talkin to me?'

## NEWTON

When the apple struck Newton's head
It felt as heavy as lead

But he yelled out with glee
This is Gravity
What a pity the poor bugger's now dead.

# PHOTOS

Me outside **36 Paola Square, Malta,**
where I was born. There's the balcony that I sometimes
slept in.

My very first group, '**The Interns with Toni Martel**'

My old buddy from way back, **Kirk St James.**
a brilliant vocalist and front man.

**"The Ghost" Me, Danny McGuire, Paul Eastment,
Shirley Kent, Terry Guy**

**The Wellington Kitch Jump Band**
Left to Right : **Bill Clarke Bass**, **John Burnett**
**Trumpet, Frank Rudge Sax, John Howells Vocals,**
**Me Drums, Vernon Pereira Gtr/vcls, Barry Lunn**
**Organ**

**Wizzard**
**Roy, Keith, Nick, Mike, Rick**
**Front: Me and Bob**

**Martin Kinch,** Our Greatest Fan. Lovely Guy. He has more photos and info on all of Roy Wood's bands than anyone in the country. Check out his website.
**www.cherryblossomclinic.freeserve.co.uk**

Old Buddy **Diz Watson,** Great Boogie Piano, and Vocals

**Bob Brady, Dave Pritchard, Dave Jinks, Me, Greg Masters.**(Dave Pritchard & Greg Masters from 'The Idle Race') Dave Jinks a friend of mine and many a Birmingham band.

**Bob Brady,Mike Burney,Martin Kinch,Me, & Nick Pentelow.**

**Richard Tandy**
Keyboards with **E.L.O**
We were in 'Organised Chaos' in the late 60's

My dear friends **Juliet & Angela.**
From the 'Frame Factory'

**Trevor Burton.**
Guitar with '**The Move**' and The Trevor Burton Band.

**Geoff Turton** of '**The Rockin Berries**'

**Me, Ken & Ian** of **(The Jive Aces)** and **Chas McDevitt,** Skiffle King.

Me with **Jim Davidson**

**Michael Dillon** owner of **'Gerry's Club'**

My old mate **Jim Broadbent** A very busy actor nowadays. We were on the road with **The Fosdyke Saga** for four months.

**Hugh Frazer**
We were in two plays together. **Teeth 'n' Smiles** and
**'England England'** He's more known as Captain
Hastings in **'Poirot'**

The lovely Joy from **'Quill'**. One of Birmingham's
finest bands

The King and I **Danny King,** singer extraordinaire.

**Pauline & Angela. Two very dear friends:** They
started out as regular punters who came to see Bob,
Nick, and myself playing, and we all stayed in touch
and remained great friends for many moons.

**Tony Kelsey**
A great guitarist with several bands including 'The Move'

**ISOSCELES**
Pat & Dave are a comedy duo with their own unique brand of humour. They are very original, and they are also accomplished actors. I sometimes work with them when we do a "*Variety Night*" gig. (They're not really heavy drinkers, only when they hear me singing) Good luck fellas.

**Karl-Howman (Brush Strokes)**

I first met Karl when we worked together on the West-End production of 'Teeth'N'Smiles'. That was 1976 ...it was a Rock musical (my first introduction to the theatre, a different gig altogether.) I'm still in touch. with Karl from time to time. I'll say this for Karl. There's nothing *flash* about him, he's a diamond geezer

**Graham Walker**

One half of the **Grumbleweeds**. I've known these guys for yonks, very funny and extremely professional. They used to be a 5 piece comedy band, but over the years they had a few changes and are now a duo and still very entertaining. Keep packing them in fellas. Sadly he is no longer with us as he lost his battle with cancer in 2014.

**Robin Colvill**
The other half of the **Grumleweeds**
There seems to be no limit to the people he can
impersonate.

**Burt Kwouk**
Taking a break from leaping on Inspector Clouseau at
the Annual Soho Ball. Another 'Gerry's Club' stalwart.
He's a mean singer too (Barber Shop harmonies his
speciality)

**Cannon & Ball.** At Great Yarmouth in 2004. Still "rockin on" "Rock on Fellas"

This is the most recent of **'The Old Horns Band'** From left....: **Me** (Bongos), **Bob Brady** (Keyboards/Vocals), **Phil Bond** (Accordion /Keyboards), **Roger Hill** (Gtr/Vocals), **Nick Pentelow** ( Saxes, Flyte), **Mike Burney** (Saxes/Flute), **Tyrone Bishop** (Bass) **and Dave Wilkes** (Drums). Apologies to Dave being a little out of shot. Sadly **Roger** and **Mike** have both passed away since. I'd like to think that they're up there in the great gig in the sky, rehearsing for when the rest of us get there. **R.I.P** fellas.

**Bob Hill, Big Albert, Me, Keith Smart**
Big Albert and I used to go to the same Gym, but I got
my money back.

Me with **Philip Jackson** ( Inspector Japp in
Poirot)

Me with **Eric Montfort** (DJ Malta) and **Tony Carr** (Maltese Percussionist)

## Published by Mirag Publications 2015

CPSIA information can be obtained at www.ICGtesting.com
Printed in the USA
LVOW04s1924290315

432482LV00030B/882/P

9 780993 187711